A DELICATE BALANCE OF REASON

Adventures In The Culture Wars

Sean Bw Parker

Seraglio Point Productions

Copyright © 2024 Sean Bw Parker

All rights reserved

No part of this book may be reproduced, or stored in a retrieval system, or transmitted in any form or by any means, electronic, mechanical, photocopying, recording, or otherwise, without express written permission of the publisher.

Cover design: Liminal Faces by Sean Bw Parker

Dedicated to

Dr. Michael Naughton

CONTENTS

Title Page
Copyright
Dedication
1   3
2   8
3   10
4   13
5   16
6   20
7   24
8   27
9   31
10   36
11   40
12   44
13   49
14   54
14   60

15	63
16	67
17	72
18	78
19	81
20	85
21	89
22	92
23	96
24	100
25	104
26	109
27	112
28	117
29	122
30	126
31	130
32	135
33	139
34	143
35	147
36	150
Acknowledgement	155
About The Author	157
Books By This Author	159

A Delicate Balance of Reason

Sean Bw Parker

1

Far Right, Transphobic and the End of the Label

'Ultimately the only power a label has is the fear of it'

The more the cancelled are condemned, the more they seem to be onto something. When Laurence Fox called out an audience member for perceived racism on BBC1's Question Time at the end of the 2010s, offers for work dried up, as the industry considered him too toxic to touch. Not long afterwards, the Black Lives Matter movement was exposed as being largely grift (as later flagged on a Kanye West hoodie).

Graham Linehan couldn't sell a script for years after coming out against the teaching of transexualism in schools, the media and co-morbidly attached entertainment industry outraged that the much feted Father Ted creator could be so apparently non-progressive. How dare he? Then the NHS-funded gender reassignment Tavistock Centre was closed, with thousands of lawsuits from now-furious transitioned youngsters against them. The Mermaids clinic was also soon under investigation for similar reasons, and Nicola

Sturgeon resigned due to her perma-evasive inability to truly define the nature of woman. Still, the BBC, Guardian et al clung on to their hoodwinked, anti-nature beliefs.

We've been spinning the news so much since the 1990s it's a wonder our heads are still on. From Tony Blair and Alistair Campbell onwards, if the media wants something to happen, it will campaign for it, and if leftist papers and broadcasters are found to have been misguided, U-turns are agonisingly hard to find. The defenestration of Matt Hancock - Health Minister at the time of the Covid pandemic - was grisly to witness. While his WhatsApp messages displayed a stunning arrogance, they also display what the public already knew: that politicians tend to be careerist, image-obsessed virtue-signallers.

Truth is thin on the ground. However trans prisoner Isla Bryson, Metropolitan policeman convicted of multiple offences David Carrick and variously accused illegal immigrants find themselves put through the New Reporting of Rape, as the term seems to somehow increasingly cover various degrees of perceived grooming, coercive control and bullying behaviour. Gender dysmorphia, negative cyclical bad habits or cultural differences will be conflated into various iterations of toxic masculinity, with the fact of actually increasing rape convictions and various forms of domestic violence being in reality 50/50 being disregarded or mentioned as a grudging afterthought.

The talents of Pulp Fiction and The King's Speech producer Harvey Weinstein, greatest twentieth century painter Pablo Picasso, and passion in art in general, are subsumed into universal print condemnation of their past sexual behaviour, alleged and tried. Men seem to be better at separating these aspects of criminology and the wider arts, with a deeper appetite for playing the ball, not the man. The bad habits of the maker can be seen in one way, and appreciation for that which they've created can be seen in another. There are likely deep-seated, naturally immutable reasons for this, buried in the primal cortex, where the male is required to reproduce without fear or favour, and will use his social position (and anything else he can find) to do so.

The radical activist tone of essentially all mainstream media considers this approach disgusting heresy, and its proponents liable to summary cancellation left right and centre. However promiscuity relates neither to rape nor 'bad character', whatever sexual assault trial processes maintain; the media increasingly assumes a narrative, and seems to consider all deviation from it deviance in itself. The flogging isn't over with cancellation or trial though, as Justice Secretary Dominic Raab's 'Community Payback' ensures that those caught on the wrong side of the culture wars are left flailing for the work in which they once trained for or were even expert.

The term 'Transphobic' has joined that of 'Far Right' in signalling the End of the Label. The progressive media gives a tag to those things of which it does not approve, whether that is supposed toxic masculinity, nationalism or extremism, but it's been shown that labelling worried mothers transphobic for not wanting their children to be taught they can transition to the other sex, few questions asked, is ridiculous.

The assault on motherhood doesn't stop there, as single mothers have historically been called council house grifters, and those choosing having a child - the most natural and obvious role for any living creature - are somehow backwards, simple-minded, or suffering from the bewilderingly patronising 'internalised patriarchy'. Coercive Control is a newer stick with which to beat men, ignoring (post-feminist writer and academic) Janice Fiamengo's theory that most allegations of this actually originate in the behaviours of women. Parental Alienation goes hand in hand with CC, as family courts around the world appear to be increasingly in league with ending paternal contact with their children when relationships break down.

With the fall of the Tavistock and its supporters ever quieter in the stinging glare of reality, will 'mental health' be the new front in the culture wars? Damaged people weaponising their often self-imposed distress in courts and employment tribunals will surely ramp up as the trans debate drifts away, with actual damage being claimed for perceived slights. If misgendering a She as a He is (or was) a sackable offence, wait until calling someone lazy, disloyal or unreliable joins them in the realms of the litigable. Who'd be a boss nowadays?

Is the institutionalised cult of Woke the new Paganism? The contempt in which its adherents seems to hold the Abrahamic religions indicates a return to the trees of the druids, with added plastic surgery, hair dye and piercings. The new puritanism has long made leftist Generation X-ers and Millennials essentially seem the new Enemies of Pleasure, until they've had a few glasses of whatever and the real self unleashes itself. The Woke might like to see themselves as multicoloured punks, but there was little moral virtue-signalling to the original 1976ers - only that which some (old) leftist journalists grafted on. Most of them were about light street criminality rather than social justice.

The fetishisation of youth indulged in by the media since the 1950s, turning with the generations, has always been a money-spinner; but nowadays its the ageing grey-haired ramblers where the money is, and whom the mainstream media is having a harder and harder time reaching (the pockets of). The great cultural relabelling continues regardless, with downblousers joining upskirters and revenge porn artists, sizing up the prohibited image collectors and domestic violence cases in prisons up and down the land, whose staff need to genuflect to the insistence of correct pronoun usage by their dysmorphic charges. In private, however, there seems to remain a presumption of 'He'.

The progressive movement and the libertarian creative make increasingly difficult bedfellows, as the polar extremes of technology and human rights versus nature become further manipulated by community-interested, monetised influences. Masculinity Studies as a course offer still seems quite a way off, but in the meantime all the sane of both sexes can ask for is a dose of heavy Individualism. Because the collective is in a troubled state. Ultimately the only power a label has is the fear of it.

2

Identity Politics and The Arts

Do you think identity politics are destroying the arts? Why is it important who made the work, isn't the quality of the work the thing? That was the argument until the #MeToo and Black Lives Matter movements at the end of the 2010s, when identity politics made a compelling yet cannily orchestrated land grab for institutions across the Anglosphere.

But that's OK I hear you say, privileged white western men have had it their own way for aeons, it's time everyone else got some of the pie, it's only fair, right? Yes indeed, and government funded diversity policies duly follow to prop up this new, commercialised form of cultural inclusion. Problem is that the music industry has been quietly 'racist' for decades, but it called this marketing demographics. The people who buy Beyonce or Coldplay in fact do mostly fit into the brackets which you'd expect.

Another thing the watching public forgets is that

awards ceremonies are at root a marketing tool, to promote work done, or that of figures who've done a lot of good (or profitable) work. When an artist, album or film manages to be both critically acclaimed and whizzo box office, the sweet spot has been hit: think Pulp Fiction (oh no hang on, produced by Harvey Weinstein). How about Arcade Fire then, massive indie band, selling millions while keeping integrity intact? Er...try again.

So the new woke morality is making a minefield of shared Western culture. The Mediterranean, Russia and the Far East countries are suffering the atrophying of liberal democratic culture-of-choice far less; not because they're any less 'advanced', but because they frame progress differently.

3

During the first world war, Mustafa Kemal Ataturk had defended the Ottoman empire against the occupying British and French forces, building the modern Republic of Turkey after the wars' end. Whilst being existentially opposed to western imperialism, Ataturk's aspirations were nevertheless clearly western-looking as he westernised the alphabet, language and clothing, and ensured the state was legally secular, a regime imposed for years with a dictatorially iron fist.

While his photograph is still everywhere in Istanbul, on note money, coins and in school books, his legacy is increasingly discussed, as they sometimes were in the advanced English classes I taught. Some thought he was a liberator, others quietly that he was an anti-Muslim elitist, and a couple of more conspiracy-minded students that he was secretly Jewish (being geographically as he was as much from Greece as from Turkey).

Anti-Semitism has always been one of those things happening outside of my sphere of awareness, and when things are like that for long enough, you are astounded when you actually encounter it. In the words of the deathless Jarvis Cocker: *'You're amazed that they exist'*. It's in reflection of all these points that comes my assertion in the belief of absolute freedom of speech, from Anjem Choudhary to Tommy Robinson, Monty Python to letterboxes.

We've seen a veritable festival of the use of the terms 'whataboutery', '(blah) apologist' etc. I remember after 9/11, those attacks were media headlines for 3-4 weeks, before other stories were allowed to return to the top of the agenda. The term 'too soon' has been a useful and polite way to let comedians and commentators know that they weren't allowed, by mutually agreed decency standards, to wittily opine just yet. Some of course didn't agree. It's almost as if international crises obliged society to run through the stages of grief before objectivity was allowed in.

In the two decades since 9/11, mainstream media has diversified beyond all recognition as social media - plus multiculturalism - have taken hold. This means that counter-perspectives are immediate, and with increasingly equal intensity, leading to huge street protests from one side while national buildings are lit up with flags of the other. I witnessed the Gezi Park riots in Turkey in 2013, where citizen and police violence led to multiple curfews and genuine social paranoia over a series of weeks and months. If there is risk of real social breakdown due to these tensions - in the UK in the context of Gaza - be wary of it being used as an excellent excuse to lock us all down again.

It can seem strange that the toxic maelstrom that is social media immediately ceases when you walk out of the front door. Depp-Heard is still raging after three years or so, people are furious about Covid, few news stories can be trusted, the personal and political have been completely mixed up, and Israel-Palestine brought real-time horror to every timeline. But if you turn off the internet on your phone and go out for a walk, the sky is still blue (or grey). The metaverse and humdrum physical world are still discrete, for most of us. I wonder - as with the personal/political - how long they will remain separate?

All the Abrahamic religions claim to be peaceful; with provisos in their texts that believers must be willing to fight or die for their God. This is similar to the de-facto nation state decree, Thou Shalt Not Kill - unless it's in the course of fighting for your country. The long argument of who has First Nation claim to the Holy Land is as unsatisfactory as chicken and egg or Big Bang theory - there are no agreed terms. If there were, it wouldn't have been Donald Trump who was the leader closest to securing a peace deal when he was in office. The sudden and horrific re-emergence conflict at least shows the West the triviality of its own new-fangled 'culture wars' - however tangentially related they might be.

4

Academic Activists, Hate Speech and the Queen

In the hours following Queen Elizabeth II's death on September 8th 2022, there was a genuine outpouring of grief from all over the world. She had been the one human constant to anybody over 70 years of age for decades, and her constitutional silence on political matters made her appear relatively uncontroversial. So when professor Uju Anya of Carnegie Mellon University tweeted that she wished the Queen an 'excruciating' death, the more understanding of those reading wondered 'Why?'

Despite the predictable tidal wave of outrage that flooded both Anya and Carnegie, she refused to apologise or retract (though the university did, quoting Anya's right to free speech in its somewhat pained response). Free speech indeed, and the right to offend, sure; but having such an angry person responsible for teaching vibrant young minds at a prestigious institute of higher education? Is it 'cancel culture' to hope that no one who wills the painful death of a 96 year old woman be allowed to continue educating others? And which student would want someone so myopically consumed with hate lecturing them anyway?

In 1997 Charles Ridenhour (or Chuck D) marketed his band's *It Takes A Nation Of Millions To Hold Us Back* album to white middle-class boys across the west. This incendiary – not to mention outrageously funky - record contained mini-lectures on all aspects of black history, from slavery to Malcolm X and Martin Luther-King, and the term racist was indeed sporadically deployed (mostly in reference to the police). Nowhere though did he personally hold one person responsible for the historical actions of many nations, in the way that did his academic successor Anya.

This is the difference between the fact-based grievance at the past affecting the future reflected in art, twentieth century style, and the feelings-based rage at perceived injustice affecting ones life choices, twenty-first century style. Progressive activist academics realised decades ago that their emasculated, intersectional, subjective, anger-based plan for this century would only happen if they could get 'em young (possibly inspired by the marketing of cigarettes in the middle of the previous one). This depended on what had become known as the 'woke' agenda not meeting insurmountable resistance. Give me control of a nation's media, and I care not who makes its laws, is a quote attributed to any number of media moguls, but its message remains the same: elected mandates are less important than winning hearts and minds.

The second a North American academic wished an excruciatingly painful death on a monarch beloved by millions of her own people around the world was its Franz Ferdinand moment. The work that hard-working rights activists had been doing for years in terms of reparations and educational acknowledgement was undone in one click of a button on Twitter.

A culture war may be better than a real one, but it's often said that hate must not win. Quite right, it mustn't - and nor must we let one-eyed grievance polarise us in a time of international mourning for many.

5

Colston, the Capitol and the End of the Righteous Jape

When the statue of Edward Colston was felled by a group of exasperated protestors and activists in the middle of the coronavirus pandemic and rolled into Bristol docks, the silent majority squirmed in their armchairs.

Colston had been a slaver from the age of empire, but problematically also gave away much of his controversially gotten wealth to educational and charitable causes. Priorities were ordered differently then, and pretty much every now successful nation had blood on its hands. King Leopold of Belgium's industrially brutal exploits in the Congo arguably put Britain's in the shade, and the Abolitionist movement found its greatest successes in Britain first.

Popular commentators from BBC television historian David Olusoga down had taken Bristol's past as their main current injustice, and the media importing of the Black Lives Matter movement, inspired by the death of George Floyd in Minneapolis, had helped inflame the Bristolian progressives into an ebullient, righteous (some might say) mob.

A few months later, Republican Donald Trump was narrowly beaten in the US election by 78 year-old Joe Biden, and Trump blamed a combination of the 'China virus' (Covid 19) and BLM as an international conspiracy between the communist Chinese government and radical leftist so-called progressives, such as Antifa (anti-fascism). A couple of weeks before Biden's inauguration, and at the height of the coronavirus' second wave (it had by that point killed over 400,000 Americans), another furiously ebullient mob, allegedly spurred on by Trump's tweets, stormed the Capitol building in Washington in an attempt to stop vice president Mike Pence confirming Biden as winner.

Lecterns were stolen, windows smashed, and men were memorably photographed in bearskins and horned helmets, standing proudly in the middle of the historical lobby. Five lost their lives in the afternoon's drama, but due to which sides' actions was a muddy field on which to play. Ex-governor and Terminator Arnold Schwarzenegger took to social media to compare the mini-putsch to Kristallnacht in 1930s Germany, when the Nazi party smashed the windows of shops owned by Jewish people in Berlin and other cities.

Where Kristallnacht was the targeting of a minority group in an burgeoning totalitarian state, the storming of the Capitol was a minority group expressing their alternative belief that power had been stolen from them by a pseudo-progressive conspiracy. More than 74 million people had voted for Trump, and they were frustrated this hadn't been quite enough to win (even if there was fairly compelling evidence about a degree of voter fraud). This exasperation, usually expressed in a democracy through protest, doesn't equate to being a 'hate group' along the lines of the (similarly democratically elected) Nazi party in mid-war Germany.

The tone of the western media, famously staffed by allegedly neo-Marxist, mixed-heritage, gender-fluid, vegan Warriors of Woke was celebratory of the felling of Colston but condemnatory of the storming of the Capitol, while at every turn pretending to be politically neutral. Their editors and managers thought that because they had been outraged for years over the tacit establishment support of figures like Colston, the silent majority would welcome the downing with whoops of joy. The reality was that the BBC was allegedly holding back on a poll over support for the Black Lives Matter protests because it was 'afraid of what it might show'.

The relatively indifferent UK public could see that the legitimate anger of one group (BLM) was being treated differently than the legitimate anger of another (MAGA, or Make America Great Again), and that this was happening along identity politic/culture war lines. The general view of the British public was that the past was a foreign country and a dangerous place, where all kinds of now-unacceptable things had once happened, in most now 'successful' countries. The view of the media left was that a statue was a physical reminder of a cruel past, which needed to be removed in acknowledgement of the sensibilities of ethnic minority people; if not by petition then by action.

The internet had made billions of views equally

valid, and exposed the politicisation of various interested gatekeepers. Establishment media was struggling to control this entirely new phenomenon, of anybody sufficiently outraged being able to instantly change the views of an already restive audience. They were simmeringly furious about everything from immigration to multiculturalism, statues to Brexit. Strongman populism was a way of funnelling this discomfort with the speed of social change, but was seen as a regressive step by most of the media. The pockets of the media where this was not seen as too retrograde a step were also demonised as the mouthpieces of Satan.

The downing and drowning of the Colston statue and the storming of the Capitol building in Washington were what once would have been called something like impassioned japes, but were now politicised and amplified into major moments of cultural change by the hyperreal processing of a thousand media streams, themselves feeding algorithmically into people's instant reactions. The leadership of the UK and the US had their work cut out in needing to reunite their newly factionalised countries, and to restore at least a modicum of trust to the political system.

6

Moral Relativism in the Court of Public Opinion

Outrage is relative. When I was teaching cultural studies in Istanbul, half of my students were blithely positive about the works of Adolf Hitler, and were amused by my own outrage at that. In return I was outraged at their mocking of the theory of evolution. It's all about whatever you've been indoctrinated to think, regardless of its veracity.

Separating the art from the artist isn't a problem for some, but is a major stumbling block for others. The fearful, cautious, neurotic, depressed or risk-averse will respond more poorly to stories of Pablo Picasso or Lucien Freud's alleged womanising than the more bold, reckless, casual, positive or risk-taking types. The latter group however also commit more violent crime, and in order to minimise this social fact, emasculation is a ready natural remedy.

The Anglosphere has been rampantly emasculating since at least the turn of the millennium, and now here we are. Hollywood actor Leonardo DiCaprio's fountain of youth, for example, has been made verboten by a semi-outraged Twitter which can't seem to bear the evolutionary fact that a successful middle-aged man might enjoy the company of younger, positive, more energetic women.

Retaining a balance of impulse reaction becomes more difficult as the shrill cries of outrage resonate around social media, and through the various channels used by those sitting on devices - not out there taking the actual risks. Then the increasingly ubiquitous Double-Bind takes over. The double-bind in social media rhetoric starts with an accusation, for example:

'You're racist.'

The response is : 'No I'm not, how dare you!' to which the original accuser replies:

'You say that because you've internalised your racism.'

Exchange racism for any other label to suit: the accused is bound by a gaslight.

Was UK Justice Secretary Dominic Raab falsely accused of bullying? He discontinued veteran radical feminist Victims Commissioner Dame Vera Baird from her position, and was suddenly besieged by over thirty allegations of being apparently 'overly-assertive'. One politico's bullying is another civil servant's perfectly justified assertiveness, and in a snitch-complaint culture mixing of the private and state-educated is going to result in a new form of behavioural sieving. Just ask ex-Home Secretary Priti Patel, found guilty of similar behaviour.

Patel's loyal boss Boris Johnson's reluctance to snitch was one of his more celebrated qualities, but it was this very unpolitical loyalty that eventually did for him when he seemed to ignore allegations of Whip Chris Pincher's drunken same-sex gropings, which proved to be the last straw for the Parliamentary Conservative Party (even if the regions largely still loved the then-PM).

Kindness-with-Benefits is the name of the game in many progressive circles, as being kind is the panacea to those with pronoun woes - at least with regards to finding the right ones - leading to the cardinal sin of misgendering a self-identifying woman with beard and balls. Meanwhile the commercialisation of sexual assault rolls on merrily as Operation Soteria, seemingly named after its US for-profit namesake, lowers the bar for the prosecution of SA in the UK, ensuring convictions go up and the radical feminists keep these kind of complaints out of the headlines – the writers of which are either other RadFems (or their facilitators in specs).

In the same way as the increasingly industrialised promulgation of sex allegation myths, Prince Harry and Amber Heard share something else in common. Written, implied and published, their deepest secrets are spatchcocked open for the public to devour like eagles at Prometheus' liver, these desperate new deities-amongst-men bound to the rock by their own alleged stealing of fire.

Will 'vexatious Self-ID' become a new offence? As identity politics becomes truly subjective, and the threat of a purely case-by-case, zero precedent legal system looms; how we feel about ourselves at any given moment – let alone the time of the alleged offence – may become paramount. The end of the belief in both Free Will and personal responsibility is nigh, as well as the necessary end of de-colonists using English as the lingua-franca. Morality is now more blurred and dependent on expedience than it's ever been.

7

How Johnny Depp and Tom Cruise Saved Hollywood

You might be thinking that after Harvey Weinstein was sent down for 23 years in the aftermath of the #MeToo movement that would be the death-knell for high quality mainstream film-making in Hollywood. After all The Weinstein Company took indie directors like Quentin Tarantino and presented them in every cinema in the world, incrementally increasing the odds through *Reservoir Dogs, Pulp Fiction, The English Patient* through to *The King's Speech* (not to mention a thousand Simpsons episodes, bringing TV's most successful comedy character to fullness in Homer, reflecting America and the wider west back at itself weekly).

So when Weinstein was finally incarcerated after years of open rumours for crimes apparently committed and crimes not, it looked like that sort of spirit of energised, integrity-driven movie production was as on the ropes as his reputation. All this ushered in a new era of casting safeguarding procedures, brilliantly satirised in Channel 4's *Adult Material,* and ultimately criticised by Slab of Yorkshire himself, Sean Bean. He said that too much safeguarding oversight killed the passion and spontaneity necessary for a good (acted) lovemaking performance, and you knew instinctively what he meant.

The days of Stanislavsky's 'Method' would appear to be up, let alone doing something like trying to re-create Marlon Brando's rape scene in *Last Tango in Paris*. Rumours abounded that *Game of Thrones* spin-off *House of Dragons* would have glimpses and snapshots of sex, rather than the full-scale shagging of the original series. Did that mean it wasn't filmed due to safeguarding, or it was edited out by queasy producers?

At the same time as all this thespo-sexual hand-wringing Johnny Depp was sitting in a US court opposite his ex Amber Heard, who a couple of years before had written a piece on domestic abuse, tacitly implicating - but not naming - him as the sole perpetrator. The Sun newspaper had won a case against his sueing for defamation in the UK; but on American soil, where cameras were allowed to broadcast from the courthouse, he fared better, being awarded $10 million damages as opposed to her $2 million. Attrition was added in the armies of bloodthirsty fans, the vast majority female/bots, slaughtering each other on Twitter. It would be a shame if either actor's career was dwarfed by such a case of domestic toxicity, played out on the world stage, but time will tell.

Following quickly in the slipstream of all this alpha activity, a memo was zapped by the Gods of Scientology to Tom Cruise in front of his wall of computer monitors, telling him to get ready to appear in a sequel to 1987's *Top Gun* (Cruise's breakout blockbuster). 'Ok,' he smiled, 'as long as we go back to basics', he might well have said.

Depp, Cruise, Miramax, Universal, the Oscars and all the rest know that the public vote with their feet on 'woke' movies, and make all the right noises, but don't want to spend their Friday evenings being lectured at from the silver screen. They get enough of that from the mainstream news. So Tom got the stripey helmet on, got the teeth out, and sexy-grinned as if his loop-the-loopy life depended on it.

The film was an enormous hit, signing the way for the reality that the movie-going public want red-meat fun, machismo, romance, derring-do and all the hokey nonsense that goes along with it. And they know it's hokey nonsense, not necessarily 'right', and they don't care. They've voted thus in elections proving this over and over the previous decade.

So it took handsome multi-millionaire alphas in the forms of Johnny Depp and Tom Cruise to turn the juggernaut of cultural woke around, in North America at least. Now, time for the print media and the broadcasters. Joe Rogan and Douglas Murray, it's over to you.

8

When the blood stops flowing, my prediction is that Rumble will have cleaned up nicely. The 'Channel of the Cancelled' may not seem very politically correct, but what watchable content is, or indeed has ever been? While there are a mixture of colours of parties in power across the world, there is overwhelming evidence that free expression is under attack in every advanced democracy. On an otherwise epochal Headliners on GB News, Lewis Schaffer repeatedly referred to his concept of 'Team World'. TW represents the progressive woke, elitist new international, headed by characters like Tony Blair, Macron and Bill Gates.

Team GB (or Team Nation) is the solo unit against this: the Brexit and populism debate again, reframed for this decade. Lewis says every news story fits into one of these camps: trans (Team World) vs anti-trans activism (Team Nation), for example. Adam Boulton's term 'broadcast ecology' is what he referred to on Newsnight, in that programme's one-sided, almost neurotic takedown of the channel. GB News' 'punk upstarts' - copyright Paul Cox - versus the delicate balance of the legacy media's grown up news.

In the realpolitik of the media, it's important to remember that however outraged we might be by stories concerning Laurence Fox, Dan Wootton or any other media figure, the algorithm Rules OK. A lot of GB News' presence is online, and they do this really well, particularly compared to other channels. All of our likes and shares go into the algorithm, making the story trend, keeping it in the headlines, and getting the numbers upon which advertisers trade.

While there's much moralising and criticism, it's a business, which is why Elon worked out a way to monetise the trolls - the more abuse you get, the more you earn. The BBC's establishment Goliath versus GB News' upstart David only exists as our creation: in the minds of the producers and editors, it's all about the algorithm.

There's a strange habit of demonising the decade before the last, until they have their own cultural tag. 1950s: staid households; 1960s: swinging miniskirts' 1970s: sleazy leather n' lino, etc. Now the 2000s are 'naughty/depraved' or something. Strange that an illegal war in Iraq, the first black president and birth of social media have all been disregarded in favour of this. Scorched earth policy? And don't even get me started on the 1980s.

At the end of the last century, there was a lot of talk about how the 21st was going to be the 'information century'. As the 19th was historically defined by wars of empire and the 20th by mechanisation and ideology, the 21st century's culture war has been a very real thing. Less blood, but similar regime change (Obama and Trump's elections, the Arab Springs, Brexit). Proxy wars in Afghanistan, Iraq, Syria and Ukraine have filled the lack of appetite for full blown international war, and instead ideological push and pull over the nature of progress reigns, played out on a million media channels, and now podcasts.

So the information century, with all knowledge at the touch of a button, is here - but the innate, natural divisions remain. The global elite are arguably trying to eradicate these differences, but individuals collectivised have decided they're not so keen. Turns out individuality is as important on a psycho-spiritual level as it was in Nietzsche's day. There will be complaints from the idealists that 'humans never learn': but the assertion of individualism isn't about learning, it's about essence. And that's what these actual Info Wars are all about.

(Scene: emergency Zoom meeting between Moloko's Roisin Murphy and her PR manager)

PR: I know that's how you feel Ros, but Spotify and Rolling Stone say that if you don't take it back they're going to take down your music and stop coverage.

RM: I don't give a fook! Women can't become men just because they say so after a month of counselling, fuckin' bollocks!

PR: That's as may be Ros, but there will literally be no more gigs or streams, as they're going to shut the whole thing down, and attack your legacy. They'll spin it as TERF stuff, I'm so sorry about this.

RM: So if I lie and apologise for not supporting their lie, we all keep workin', but if I don't we all suffer because I'm trying to tell the truth? Jesus H. Christ.

RM: Sorry Ros, you're getting it.

RM: Just put the fuckin' apology out, eejits the lot o' ya. (Pours out a full tumbler of whiskey.)

9

Dan Wootton, Media Neurosis and 'Diversity'

'The activists are in a permanent state of adolescence, and the adults are paying the price'

GB News presenter and experienced tabloid journalist Dan Wootton was recently accused by leftist website Byline Times of potential video sex extortion, heavily quoting Wootton's ex-partner.

This came hot on the heels of veteran BBC News presenter Huw Edwards having 'no case to answer' to a similar type of allegation, but being outed by his wife after Jeremy Vine and other media types said it was 'bringing the BBC to its knees', so to fess up. These were not long after *This Morning*'s face-of-the-ages Philip Schofield, having previously come out as gay, was exposed as having an 'unwise but not illegal' affair with a young ITV staffer.

While Wootton will likely never be forgiven by an army of Johnny Depp supporters who hold him personally responsible for their hero losing his libel battle against his old paper *The Sun*, he (and all the others mentioned above) are a product; empathy as to their situation from this angle is irrelevant.

We think we know them as they are public-facing, well-mannered and ambitious, but they are creations of the *Simulacra* - philosopher Jean Baudrillard's term for the fantasy-reality we create through celluloid and related technology. Is the science behind the magic, or magic behind the science? At what point does the private person become the product, and when are they - or we - allowed to switch off in a culture that now never does?

The 1960s featured a cultural revolution due to previous generations being too restrictive, class-bound and warlike. The 2010s and 20s' (thus far just attempted) woke revolution has been led by the (great) grandchildren of that revolution: but the Boomers did nothing explicitly 'wrong' to cause this.

While footballer Ryan Giggs was cleared of long-standing domestic abuse charges due to his ex-partner withdrawing charges due to 'pressure', *Brass Eye* and *The Thick of It* producer Armando Iannucci revealed that the BBC had reinstated actor Chris Langham on the latter show, previously convicted of keeping prohibited images. The fact that the BBC decided that once a sentence has been served - whatever the accused's plea - the sentence is served, is admirable in the current conviction-on-allegation culture.

The activists are in a permanent state of adolescence, and the adults are paying the price. No midlife crisis goes unpunished, and every high profile male is as likely as the next to see his entire legacy binned. Toxic masculinity is in fact feminised masculinity, as the public sees the crime of rape as actually MORE serious than do the activist-feminists; who see rape as almost all hetero sex, and conflate sexual assault and non-violent rape allegations on a regular basis. Must be the patriarchy - which, contrary to the messaging, is now to all intents and purposes a matriarchy, due to the prevalence of women in positions of power across most industries.

When it comes to bloodthirsty social media trolls, seeing all human behaviour in black and white terms and blocking before anyone has a chance to defend themselves - as if there's any point anyway - is it Asperger's or arrogance? The 2010 Equality Act has enabled many with psychological conditions to be promoted to powerful positions within myriad institutions, and consequently the social discourse has become less balanced, less nuanced, and more childishly moralistic. It's almost as if no one is responsible for their instant emotional reactions any more, and to ask if there's a deeper reason behind them would be somehow 'hateful'.

On the subject of not burning down the past in this rush to monomaniacal scorched-earth, it's almost as if the British cultural habit of letting madness prevail quietly - then cleaning up afterwards with muttered observations behind hands - has been given new horizons upon which to ponder. Neutrality as a virtue has become a real challenge, as attempted slurs such as *'centrist dad'* or *'fascist enabler'* circle. In the creative algorithmic economy you're more likely to be put in prison for *not* having principles or a stance than for having them, and hypervigilant social media jackdaws will make sure that no response goes unnoticed.

The culture industry has gone from the scarcity model of the past to the 'just attract attention/impact' model of the present, at the same time that positive discrimination has become as culturally repressive as upper class privilege. In separating the art from the allegation, corporate governance + artificial intelligence = the New Authoritarianism, leading to the current situation where such social commentary art-as-relevance can no longer meaningfully exist.

Is it possible to be indoctrinated into a sort of anti-free speech dogma? The kids and their digital fingerprints don't think so, as they turn away shy from any controversial project, lest its influence infect their future careers. This is a recipe for bland art, and cowed creative spirits. In the era of new bonds being formed - within the endless remixing of identities - in the past the Right were arrogant and entitled, which is why many would vote against them; now they are humbled in cultural opposition.

The art of happiness lies in analysing oneself less: stop being that Proud People Pleaser, and say what you were feeling just before you were exposed for doing so. Just beyond identity politics and meritocracy still lies nepotism; professional mobility within the media class is dead; woke is essentially religion; and diversity, equity and inclusion policies ensure only produce bland, hegemonic and non-engaging art.

Maybe that's why we're so keen on feeding our household names to the lions? Or that's definitely why their internal score-settling is so engaging. Baudrillard and Dan Wootton be damned, the simulacra is way more entertaining than a million mixed-race family adverts in high-def, teeth-whiter-than-snow youngsters - and nary a happy, white middle-class couple in sight.

10

The Comedians Assert

I did an interview with Paul Cox, cancelled columnist of the Portsmouth News and GB News *Headliners* regular, on the channel's second anniversary. Paul very much speaks the truth as he finds it, and is as surprised as any other soft centre right-leftist child of Blair to have found himself labelled *'far right'* in recent times, possibly due to his position on the show. It sometimes feels one needs to be discovered buried in a paupers' coffin in Highgate Cemetery next to Karl Marx with an icepick between the ribs not to be dubbed far right in the current climate.

HL also features Simon Evans as a regular host, the occasional Radio 4 guest of the years delivering his wise literary anecdotes and alternative takes of the following morning's papers with customary eloquence. Then there is the formidable Leo Kearse, a towering slab of Icelandic-blooded Scottishness, unafraid to stand in what *The Guardian* and a million Twitter wonks would no doubt label bigotry; but as he will fearlessly point out is in fact contemporary British reality.

The Graun's most tenacious critic on the show is Nick Dixon, a stand up of both faith and Jordan Peterson impersonations who has no time for the jiggery-wokery of the legacy media. Accusations of rightist bias from that media are way off mark, as Josh Howie – charismatically bearded Jewish north Londoner – and cool head Steve N Allen jostle reasonably comfortable along gently leftish lines.

There is an assumption in the Leg.Med that GBNews' core audience are disaffected white middle-aged males, and while there are plenty of them increasingly engaged, there are just as many if not more disaffected females out there, of all ages and mindsets. This is borne out on GB's impressive Twitter/X tie-in, intelligently linking MuskWorld with its terrestrial reach – and regulars Diane Spencer and Cressida Wetton wink out at them knowingly enough.

Though the audience is far more diverse in terms of background and perspective than these sex divides indicate, Diane as an ex-schoolteacher often references what used to be called mainstream ideas with a classiness echoed in Cressida, who brings a welcome balance and objectivity to the stranger reaches of the culture wars. Because it can't be avoided that the culture wars are Headliners' bread and butter, and low-hanging comedic fruit. But as one of the show's trailers says, when the establishment has gone crazy, you need some crazy to handle it.

Have I Got News For You and *Mock the Week* would be Headliners' 'stablishment (copyright Michelle Dewberry) reference points, but here is where the difference becomes both nuanced and crucial. Those shows pretend(ed) to be cutting edge and dangerous, but they're truly not: HL is, just by dint of telling the truth as to how things actually are, rather than what they *look like*.

Exquisitely balanced host Andrew Doyle – whose brilliant *Free Speech Nation* seems very much HL's sister show – may need to pull his errant guests back to reasonableness, and anarchic New Yoiker Lewis Schaffer may feign disinterest in essentially all British papers, but it's through those idiosyncrasies that the team asserts themselves.

The hands continue to stretch across the water with immaculately coiffured, veteran gay Scott Capurro, before the elastic band snaps to send us hurtling towards Roger 'don't call him Bob' Monkhouse, with his Harry Hill-meets-Richard Vobes in a *Carry On*-surgery idiom. This is what diversity of opinion and background actually look like, along with a reminder that comedians are probably the most unpredictable individuals roaming around the community.

As the post pinned to the top of Leo's Twitter has read for some time, cancel culture – or rather the threat of it, which is just as bad – has been chronic in comedy for some time, and that's why HL is so needed. You don't have to be a rampant Berlusconi or Le Pen enthusiast to be painted as a far right extremist these days, but that experiment by certain BBC and Graun types recently backfired, as they realised they were tarring utterly normal, regular people, who immediately mocked it to the rafters.

It is to they that HL, and more broadly GBNews, is catering – and long may they remain bonkers, since the extra material is surely always welcome.

11

While Twitter/X is a receptacle for the bored, the mentally ill, the depressed and short-on-work journalists, it is also, as Lord Musk decrees, currently the 'town square' of ideas. The problem is these ideas are often presented as political polemic, rhetoric, and ungrounded assertions. Something peer reviewed by two people who are politically aligned with the author is not a peer review, it's persuasive pamphleteering.

Then there are the responses, which range from the snarky, to the snide, with the occasional moral support or good-faith curiosity, like water in the desert. These responses are increasingly the signs of the undamaged, or those who don't spend that much time online. But very little swearing, interestingly. Even in the most horrible arguments, and even in this (occasional) hellhole, there's an acknowledgement that 'Oh just go to fucking hell you absolute motherfucking arsehole' means you might have lost the argument.

Cultural appropriation is a good thing. Culture becomes richer and deeper by integrating other influences with which it comes into contact. The Rolling Stones directly interpreted the American blues, a fact usually acknowledged more by Keef Richards than Mick Jagger. Paul Simon's Graceland was an evergreen work of genius, fully integrating the dynamics of South Africa's Lady Black Mambazo into Simon's own impeccable narrative style. While pioneering cubism, Picasso was sufficiently moved by the simplicity of tribal African masks to graft them as faces of the prostitutes in his Demoiselles D'avignon, thereby defining the ethos of 20th century modern painting.

That cultural appropriation has been so captured in our progressive century is the inverted 'Stay in your lane'ism of academic identititarians, hostile to imaginative enrichment, skewering power principles into every beautiful thing. 'Take mine, I'm glad you like it, it's yours to do with what you will.'

~

Trans-activist sceptic as I am, I find the 'new misogyny' label applied to some trans people tricky. As if the highly lucrative political feminism relentless attacking of masculinity wasn't bad enough, certain elements of that same ideology see 'transwomen' using female spaces as a woman-hating act. There may be a handful of nutters doing this, but I can't imagine misogyny is a driving force. They just don't see why they should be excluded, even when they clearly should be. (I strongly oppose biological males competing in female sports, and anything sexual being taught to young children, just to clarify.)

I agree with Alice Cooper that trans is a fad, blown up by a media that absolutely, almost fiscally loves the subject - but the escalation of transitioning teens is a testament to the horrifying nature of social contagion. But sexist behaviour? I don't think so; a handful with gender dysphoria, and a generation of uncomfortable kids being encouraged that they might be in the wrong body, and that they might be happier if they 'faced' that.

~

It's been more than three years since Laurence Fox was ejected from the British acting establishment for calling out what he saw as an audience members' racism on BBC's Question Time. Since then he's founded The Reclaim Party, starred in My Son Hunter, turned presenter with his Friday night show on GB News and grown a huge following on Twitter/X. He recently heard that the courts would not be supporting a complaint against him surrounding a 'paedophile' retort, signifying a growing support for his anti-woke stance.

Dr Shola has a similar race-based notoriety, regularly being called a 'race-baiter' by viewers infuriated by her constant pulling focus on the problem of 'whiteness'. This ran through subjects such as the death of the Queen last year, and now with the conviction of Lucy Letby, claiming that she would have been caught sooner were she black. Yet still Shola crops up on This Morning or The Jeremy Vine Show on a regular basis. Free speech, of course. But why is Laurence defenestrated for calling out what he sees as racism, while Shola seems to increase her appearances by doing similar?

12

Excavating the Dinosaurs of the Cancel Culture Revolution

(Botriler Archaeology)

Most ambitious British parents have historically wanted the apples of their eyes to somehow get to Oxford or Cambridge universities, by hook or by crook. They used to have a unique appeal as the elites of the elites, the dynamism of Harvard and Yale with less emphasis on the money, it being assumed that part of life would probably follow naturally. In recent years however it has become clear that these venerable old gatehouses have been taken over by 'Woke' liberal progressives, with a turn of mind belying the very idea of classical liberalism.

Oxbridge has become nothing to aspire to if these parents (and the prospective young victims) in any way value free expression. The young, often North American research students being imported to change the old, hallowed ways bemoan what they see as a traditional, conservative atmosphere, while those same 'Conservatives' feel a disquiet they may not utter at having been obliged to genuflect to the mixed-heritage, gender-fluid, green veganism of their old institution's new religion.

If you question any of this you are mocked, de-platformed, cancelled, then fired, under the aegis: 'This conversation is over'. The New Degenerate Art is now to be found in dark corners of the Internet, the scabrous young, impressively uncowed, producing material that is quickly becoming 'unmentionable' as they swerve, ignore or smash the Overton Window, constantly scanning them like a transparent mosquito with a 'report' button.

The best way to deal with these new degenerates is to label them conspiracy theorists, extremists, sex offenders or terrorists – none of this needs to be supported in fact, just in implication. This is because, as in 21st century politics, perception is everything. Change the multi-screened perception, change the reality. Vive La Revolucion.

The word 'Sense' is another that has been cancelled by the postmodern mandarins of the lexicon, sitting cross-legged with scissors in hand, headphones in ears. To them, Common Sense now means traditionalism, Nonsense means denial, Sense of Proportion means condescension and Sensuality means deviance. If the anti-colonialist sentiment is going to really gain pace, its adherents will also need to adopt a new language (as surely the English language is presumably yet another tool of the evil imperial patriarchy).

Beyond the New Puritanism lies a place where both genders/sexes (you know what I mean) and all races will coexist relatively happily - as they always have done, to a greater or lesser extent - with a resolution to live in the present and think about the future rather than some victimhood-obsessed past towards which they are perpetually being encouraged.

This encouragement comes from a certain class of academic activistas knowing that the best way of achieving cultural change is in getting 'em young; ends justifying the means, and it not mattering how that be achieved. Enlightenment principles of science, art, tolerance and humanism are thrown onto a bonfire of agreed terms, ignited by humblesnark comments on social media, designed to inflame and catalyse.

The New Libertarians (see Boris Johnson) vs The New Puritans (see Keir Starmer) resemble the Cavaliers vs the Roundheads of history, mid-blue suits and notable hair taking the place of feathered fedoras and horned helmets, rowing in Parliament about who didn't out Jimmy Savile - while the still-living Jonathan King howls into the void on Twitter, his kitsch odyssey of a cultural past cancelled by a secretly Oscar Wilde-hating New Orthodoxy.

Whatever stands in the way of the great homogenisation must be cancelled – or at least made 'accountable'. White intersectionality is ignored, the vast array of indigenous minds of the UK and their cultural embeddedness denied and mocked on a regular basis, as the BBC laughs at traditional nationalism and urbane metropolitans describe almost any naturally occurring male instinct as somehow deviant.

The symbolic principles of the Union Jack are

regularly in question, classic of British design though it is generally considered. Laurence Fox - once cancelled but now seemingly beyond such worldly concerns - turned tables on the woke police who were going to arrest a member of the public for retweeting an image of the rainbow Pride flag, turned into a swastika shape as a comment on the increasingly punitive actions of parent org Stonewall (once a genuine 'Safe Space' for the gay community).

Prince Andrew - neither charged nor convicted of having sex with a seventeen year old he had apparently been told was on work experience - was cancelled following an interview with Emily 'Zelda off Terrahawks' Maitlis on BBC2's Newsnight, with every media outlet in the UK slagging his performance in true Simpsons style: 'Worst interview ever'. (A body language expert later said that there was no indication that Andrew was lying in any of his answers.)

Fluency and beauty biases are rife, as while it is difficult to get airtime as a white heterosexual male in the post-Title IX/Donald Trump era, it is just as difficult to become a spokesperson for women if you're a bit frumpy. These Gammons and Karens are the dinosaurs of the cultural revolution, their bones being tossed about by Stanley Kubrick's apes in 2001 as the children of Year Zero froth in the corners of their mouths about another dud being cancelled, no-platformed or convicted for Hate Speech.

The Indigenous Mind of the funny shaped islands of Britain goggles on, eyeballs extended on stalks atrophying around the Hebrides, the taut elastic in serious danger of snapping back on itself and doing serious damage. The basement oligarchy of a thousand paid Twitter trolls and Russian snarkbots upending agreed cultural norms in favour of the new language of unmandated gibberish is festooned in gold, its vajazzle glinting in the red-dotted reflection of a received notification.

The science of 'evil atmospheres' is as unexamined as the politics of a pub punch-up, the activistas watching on amused as the trolls tear each other limb from limb, safe in the knowledge that each time the media cycle turns, a wing of it chips off a bit of the old establishment. A thread can turn from jolly and nice in a turn of phrase, the corpses of Coleridge and Tennyson waiting a week to joust in the letters pages of *The Times* reanimated with added smiley faced emojis - as at least we're reminded of the power of language (as long as the algorithms agree with what a c*nt is).

The beomheards and bumblebee onesies of a thousand botrilers wait to cancel another old pop star accused of fondling an anonymous young woman in 1973, as the attritional progress of the cultural revolution rolls forward, one vastly exaggerated scenario at a time. Whether UCAS is screening the Oxbridge hopefuls parents' application forms for diversity quotas of those who identify as they/thems in who gets in on clearance is a matter only a closed-door tribunal will increasingly be able to answer.

13

The New Morality and The Arts

From conceptual fine art to neo-criminology via the #MeToo movement, morality in the arts has been on a strange journey in the 21st century thus far.

The years may roll by, but the music doesn't die, and some never treated music as an industry anyway. Increasingly nothing existed, as vinyl became streaming, and David Bowie's prediction of music becoming as easy to access as turning on a tap came true, but still we slipped into one another.

With this increasing new absence of physicality, perception management became a new spin-based art-form, perfected by the likes of New Labour's Alastair Campbell. Superseding this, living with integrity began to become an artistic prerequisite. Still, if there was any area of contemporary culture where *Safety Third* should be a guiding principle, it was surely in the arts.

Galileo was upended as the social media revolution ensured that individualism and narcissism were not the same thing, and the sun of the internet started to revolve around the Earth of the consumer. A new duck-faced army of empowered young victims were groomed by media activists into a neo-political feminism that had been consumed by adolescent messaging. Meanwhile masculinity had become elderly, and equality feminism had become comfortably middle-aged.

Commentators from Janice Fiamengo to Bettina Arndt were screaming that feminism was not always a bad thing - it just needed to grow up, as these new forms of entitlement were losing it much ground. Jordan Peterson, Matt Walsh and Andrew Tate were garnering huge audiences of both sexes, as they pointed to example after example of where toxic gynocentrism had become more important than any other literary message in any given work.

Political feminism was confidently setting itself against human nature in the tradition of the progressive left, as witnessed almost hourly in the deeply misandric tweeting of family court barrister Charlotte Proudman - sculpting out for herself a new niche as Presentable Man-Hater-At-Law. The new cavaliers and imperialists were lining up in the culture wars, as they saw the Roundheads of the global woke hegemony surging blue-haired over the horizon.

New(ish) media characters such as Laurence Fox and Calvin Robinson were heading up a sort of Heteronormative Revolt, frustrated as they were that the now-woke establishment was continuing to gaslight culture by perpetually claiming it was the resistance. The individualist howl got louder with the lockdown-era birth of GB News, its patriotic free speech brief already misrepresented while it was still in the womb. There are many other ways to restrict free speech other than just the law – which is expensive and should always be a last resort – and power-feminists sitting at the levers of power were ramping up the pushing of them.

Degenerate Art versus degeneracy itself became an unspoken dog-whistle in press reports, as transgender civil servants spaffed millions of public money up the media wall in an attempt to get the public to agree that grass was not in fact green. The (real) Nazis had banned the 'degenerate art' of artists such as Marcel Duchamp, and would have done the same to proto-conceptual artists such as Joseph Beuys or Tracey Emin. The new mavens of internationalist gender-fluid, mixed-race, environmental veganism would be more likely to frug to the 'found art' of Fatboy Slim than chin-stroke to the readymades of Duchamp; but all tastes became interchangeable in the postmodern slew.

Interactive screens seemed to become something to aspire to with age, as children were either as compulsively stuck to them in sensurround as were their parents: with the additions of peer bullying and the endless generational trauma of adolescence, itself increasingly weaponised by social justice-obsessed child-adults.

Goal oriented thinking contained ever more empty successes, as lifestyle and attitude neo-gurus such as Gwyneth Paltrow and Meghan Markle took massive pay packets to flog positive thinking mixed with identity victimhood. They would chalk up the next pay packet, sourced from a captive-aspirational female audience, on affirmative thinking: *'I visualised it as true, and it came true'*.

Baroness Michele Mone allegedly did something similar with millions of taxpayer funds in the procurement of unusable PPE during the pandemic - but it was OK, because she was achieving what she had set out to do. She had *'just gone out there and done it'*. This kind of conceptual gerrymandering was fine, but if the same 'Will It True' ethos were applied to a subject such as indigenous culture of the British Isles, say, the preacher would be stoned into oblivion.

Can (and should) the likes of Mone be rehabilitated? Rehabilitative art is championed by the justice reform left, but when actual artistic expression is expressed, safeguarding concerns will be triggered all over the sisterhood, as alarmed curators raise red flags in an ecosystem of 'Be Kind'-informed suffocation.

In A Tale of Two Aspies, Greta Thunberg and Elon Musk are the putative Anthony and Cleopatra of the algorithmic electronic culture wars, as the black-and-white thinking morality of their messaging backgrounds some grand male/female-style existential drama. It forever seems that South African Musk is constantly on the verge of tweeting something like: 'Critical race theory will lead to supported voluntary repatriation', but his non-joint holding, typing hand seems to just about stop him in time.

Should voice training ads be flagged up as Protected Characteristic infringements? Everything else is weaponised - strangely rarely ageism nor regionalism. It seems that the acquired expressive art of received pronunciation is one area in which a hierarchy of perceived quality still reigns supreme. It's hard to cancel a RADA-trained vintage actor if he can't even be selected for a role due to his perceived white male able-bodied heteronormativity in the first place. Clearly new territory to be staked out there for the cultural revolutionaries we have so come to so know and love.

With the recent double-cancellation of Father Ted creator Graham Linehan at the now fully captured Edinburgh Fringe because of his views on Trans activism, choirs being told not to sing Tom Jones' murder ballad *Delilah* and bawdy classic *Fat Bottomed Girls* being removed from Queen's evergreen *Greatest Hits*, the arts are tottering beneath the weight of histrionics on Twitter/X being listened to by a similarly captured media hegemony.

A post-Covid, post-Brexit, post-#MeToo cultural lightening is on its way, you can hear it all over. Art is the cathartic reflection of good, bad but vitally human in creative, amoral form. Like 'campaigning journalism' in the News, progressive messaging has no place within this primal expression: the sooner it is hounded out, the better.

14

The Gaslighting of Jordan Peterson: I generally can't bear neologisms, but the term 'gaslighting' is increasingly useful. It means making someone doubt the reality of their position by bad faith argument techniques: making someone crazy. We see it online every day. Justin Troudeau's establishment is gaslighting Jordan Peterson for what they call his 'unprofessional public messaging'.

This translates as its fury that 1. Peterson won't go along with the State position that sex can be changed at will, and 2. He's very popular for frankly speaking his mind. Gaslighting cares not for the truth however, as witnessed daily in 'woke' responses to criticism. Many progressive positions don't rely on logic, practicality or human nature, so the arguments tend to resort to insult, ad-hominem, 'hurt feelings' or 'be kind'. That these last two have also become gaslighting is what is destroying the pragmatic centre-ground, and can make Peterson look furious. Well, he's furious because of the gaslighting. It's practical reality (old right) vs idealistic wishful-thinking, refereed by - you guessed it, gaslighting. So, a helpful word yes, but also a horrible one.

Speaking of religion, if a Jehovah's Witness or

Mormon comes to the front door or stops me in the street, I'll possibly have a polite but brief conversation, then go on my way. If they push it, I'll respond less politely than before. Exactly the same thing with trans/woke missionaries.

(In Victorian London, Dr Shola's PR team call her into their offices)

PR: 'Dr Shola, you haven't written anything for *The Times* for a few weeks, and they've been in touch to tell us they always sell more copies when you do'.

Shola: 'The Times are a by-product of imperial slavery. Do better. Be better'.

PR: 'Anyway there's been another murder of a prostitute in Whitechapel, and we've got a great name for what's going on, "Jack The Ripper". Could you put something together for us?'

Shola: 'Are any of these prostitutes BLACK?'

PR: 'Er...'

Shola: 'Never mind, I'll do it. Stay offended. Educate yourself..'

(PR leaves as Dr Shola continues in the same vein for some minutes).

~

What is Right-Wing? I was brought up in a left-wing family, but have considered myself apolitical since I was about 17. I have voted for a different political party in every election I've been eligible to vote. I might be the definition of a 'floating voter', as I decide based on what I think the country needs at the time, rather than on historical 'loyalty'. Social media seems to have made the pragmatism of this position almost impossible.

While I still consider myself politically neutral, observers who consider themselves 'progressive' would no doubt claim I'm right-wing, as I tend to post or repost along artistic, free speech or anti-'woke' lines. That progressive woke positions have gone too far is borne out by the fact that progressives say things about which the mainstream are worried, i.e. teen transitioning in schools, aren't happening, despite overwhelming evidence to the contrary.

Party and identity politics have become interchangeable, and there seems to be no party which represents my stance: culturally libertarian, fair taxation, pro-NHS, anti-death penalty, pro-rehabilitation, pro-tradition, pro-equal rights. But because I enjoy GB News' Headliners and the Spectator interviews of Winston Marshall, apparently I'm right-wing, far right. Ok, whatever you say.

I find it interesting (if not a little amusing) that the terms Woke, TERF and Gammon, originally coined by the progressive left, have somehow been co-opted by the 'new right'. What CAN we do about this unacceptable re-appropriation of language? Not unrelated I have no problem with people droppin' their g's when they speak - I don't tend to criticise anyone's speaking style - but why does it sound so unusual when both Sadiq Khan and Priti Patel do it? I can't think of anyone else in public life who does this.

Comedy is (actually) the new Punk Rock, at last. For years marketing firms have been saying things such as 'comedy is the new rock n' roll', in an attempt to get punters interested in their production lines of public lecture. With Father Ted creator Graham Linehan being cancelled - along with the whole of the Comedy Unleashed lineup - at Leith Arches at the Edinburgh Fringe festival, the artform finally justifies the tag.

Linehan, along with a handful of others, has had the courage to go against another heavily-marketed dominance narrative: that being that children can have their problems solved by puberty blockers, breast/penis removal etc. The comedy stage is possibly the last remaining platform where humans can call out anything about which they might have questions - but apparently not any more, if it's framed by a tiny minority of online activists as 'hateful'. Well it's not Streatham Skinheads trying to aim scobs straight into the mouth of an onstage Johnny Rotten, but the comparison stands.

There has been a gradual, years-long takeover in the creative arts across the West. New music - boring; publishing - preachy; TV and film - diversity obsessed. Comedy is the last bastion of sanity, the communication of human to human, glass in hand. God bless Graham Linehan and Comedy Unleashed.

For years there was a naff schoolboy joke: 'I'm a lesbian, I fancy girls!', and there was much merriment. Andrew Doyle's Free Speech Nation remembered this in absurdam, as bearded men from Scotland to Mexico were frocking up and calling girls transphobes if they didn't want to sleep with them. A cunning trick - meanwhile David 'Ringo' Starkey made Ofcom spoosh their Sunday evening Baileys with a rare outing of the evergreen: *'Poofs, Andrew, they're called poofs'*.

I think we're heading for a critical point where more males have been accused of something - relabelled as serious - than haven't. The 70s/80s cliche 'All Men Are Rapists/Stalkers/Abusers' will have been achieved by stealth, not reality - and then what?

Apparently England's Women did quite well in the World Cup. Having always been 'sports marginal' at best, my interest in watching most is aesthetic. I genuinely marvel at the human body and concentration, free of politics or external conceptualism, fixated on the balletic intensity of self-maximisation. When I watch sports, from football to tennis to skiing, I'm wondering at the achievement in others that I cannot - and do not desire to - do. This is beyond sex divides, it's about like-against-like athletic and psychological competition. All Sports Matter, simply because of their physical honesty, and performative beauty. Well done the Lionesses.

There exists in any police force a number of nasty bullies, to put it politely, but there is also a larger group who engage in cathartic, job-surviving 'banter'. This is at odds with a College of Policing - receiving its guidance from ideological activist academics - which believes that being 'woke' is being kind and progressive, rather than the neo-authoritarianism it has increasingly been shown to be.

These latter elements have made the British police akin to a live-action version of Twitter/X. Events have shown what happens when vaguely written Equality Act directives clash with equally arbitrary 'Hate Speech' guidance. The word 'reasonable' crops up time and again in UK law - and it's been doing some unsustainably heavy lifting. My one lingering question after the (absolutely justified) Lesbian-grandmother-autistic-girl palaver is: Is the term 'Lesbian' a homophobic slur? Because I'm sure Julie Bindel etc. are demanding we call them this.

14

Diversity of Thought and the Media

There is an increasing amount of diversity of background in the media, but no real diversity of thought – an area over which the person involved actually has some influence and choice. When you're in the public eye, some people hate you, and some people are paid to hate you. If you're more interested in the reasons why something happened than in what actually happened, the postmodern British court of the media - let alone law – probably isn't for you.

In the same manner that humanity treated the physical consequences of nuclear or atomic weapons, it needed to treat algorithms – in relation to psychological effects, at least. There is a suspicion that some of the progressive-minded want to make 'competition' as taboo as cannibalism or incest, in pursuit of what they see as a fair society. Prisons don't need to be utterly brutal for people not to want to be there for very long. The main privation is in being sent there at all.

Public (or private) schools prepare pupils for the rough and tumble of public life in a way that modern comprehensives, with their 'all bad behaviour comes from good intentions' and 'everyone must win a prize' ethos, don't. Disappointment and claims of psychological abuse are rife in one, less so in the other. A young woman on the radio recently said that critical thinking had become 'a new currency' for her generation. As much as this might seem like a victory for the social sciences, they shouldn't get too obsessed: that way puritanical absolutism tends to lie.

Helen's Law is another problematic example of postmodern justice, of the law essentially making it up as it goes along. Just because the media and police say someone is guilty doesn't mean that they are. How is a prisoner supposed to say where a body is buried if s/he didn't commit the crime in the first place? The power would be near completely in the hands of the spurious and unproven. Why is it acceptable to presume 'bad character' from the past of the defendant, but not for that of the accuser?

Many allegations have transgressed from once being seen as serious crimes to being a hot topic in the culture wars. ACAB? All Cops Aren't (necessarily) Bastards: some are ideological virtue-signalling emotioneers. 'Unsure' is far more attractive than 'totally decided'. Societal cues have utterly scrambled this evolutionary fact. Mistakes made? Most aren't going to sign up to identitarianism now any more than they wouldn't sign up to Scientology at any other time.

The tension used to be between religion and science. Now it's between religion and the media. If you look back over your most treasured memories, I'll bet if nature isn't front and centre, it's definitely in the background, or at least nearby. Historically, discourse about Being would be relatively confined to the subject of Being. Now Being needs to be lumped in with culture to say anything people want to hear. What people want to hear thus directs the discourse (as the market knows well).

The dinosaurs vs. the precariat, the British vs. overstatement, denial vs. denialism, prejudice vs. presumption – identitarianism runs through all of them like an iron thread. In the hands of postmodern justice and the media, this thread has become rusted to the point of fracture.

15

The Rise and Fall of the Album as Artform

Winter 1980, and Adam Ant stares out from the 12 by 12 inch glossy cardboard square in a box in the burgundy flock-wallpapered dining room of a rural Devonshire house. His *'Kings of the Wild Frontier'* album is for now eclipsing a fascinatingly drawn ink on white of *Revolver* by The Beatles, another mysteriously powerful artwork whose contents does exactly what it says on the tin. Two musical pioneers, leading separate cultural charges 15 or so years apart, jostling anarchically for attention amidst Beethoven and Gilbert O'Sullivan.

My pre-teens elder brother and I would recklessly pull the exciting black vinyl from the covers and haphazardly bang them onto the struggling turntable, a patient housekeeper entertaining every existential need the two boys had for soaking up every moment of new sound and harmony they could discover. Adam and Lennon would move to The Stranglers and Eric B and Rakim, as the postmodern world of technicolour audio opened up in the middle of the countryside before them.

A couple of years later, beneath Grongaer hill and

Dylan Thomas' Golden Grove, the Sugar Loaf mountain and Brecon Beacons, Fine Young Cannibals, Terence Trent D'arby and The Cure would hove into the view over the bleak valley horizons, swinging guitars and tantalising haircuts in place of swords or pikes. Their message from the East was concealed in cassette tapes, fragile palm-sized boxes which would regularly break trough frenetic teenage over-opening, let alone the HB pencil 'recovery technique', which would have to be illustrated to be explained. Safe to say the magnetic tape the sound was recorded on had a fairly limited shelf life, and the ghetto blasters of the 80s would regularly churn and shred it up like a million mini-Watergates to the invigorating refrains of Guns n' Roses' *Appetite for Destruction*.

I soon started working at a nearby antiques shop, and collecting dust on top of my bureau there was an old 8-track player. This obscure device enabled me to regress to the early 60s as baggy then led into the 90s. These strange, mini UFO-type objects led me to discover the explorations of early Santana's 'Abraxas' and a certain David Bowie's nursery rhyme-like mid sixties debut. Good old Radio One would jolt me back to early 90s reality – though vinyl was living hand in hand with cassette at this point as the rest of Bowie's 70s cornucopia of delights opened up by vinyl, joss-stick and no small amount of Thunderbird, Marlboros and White Lightning cider some evenings.

The mid-90s arrived in a burst of cynical energy and music industry mega-profits, as the major labels adopted Britpop and bought-out or co-opted indie labels and contracts. The 'indestructible' CD was at peak sales, and Blur, Oasis, Take That and The Spice Girls were raking it in for the fatcats – whilst the performers apparently didn't fare too badly from the deals either.

The industry was a well-oiled machine at this point, and you could somehow smell that with the endless regurgitating of ideas. CDs weren't in fact indestructible. I remember easily smashing quite a few. The approach to the millennium was when the fetishisation of the album as desirable object floundered, as it appeared that new ideas had dried up, and they had become another source of revenue in an increasingly manipulative corporate business model. Pricing them upwards of £15 a pop might have been the proverbial straw for many.

Rumours of something called the Interweb were abound, and Bowie early informed us that it would *'change everything'*, and music would be as easy to access as *'turning on a tap'*. Original pirate file-sharers Napster led this nu-punk revolution, while the record industry labelled it theft and heavy electric gods of the enormodromes Metallica sued the young tech maestros. This was the point at which the corporate model crumbled: music became democratised, the gate-keepers were sidelined and ignored, tunes were everywhere and scarcity evaporated.

File-sharing became paid downloads, these lost traction pretty quickly, then social media and shared playlists became the thing. Conceptualised, packaged albums delivered from the ivory tower of EMI, and all the more mysterious and glamorous for it, were replaced by half a million YouTube videos watched by about 100 family, friends and well-wishers. Major labels became unwilling to invest in new talent as they were losing money, and as always has been the case, radio play needed to generally be paid for (payola) and press stories published through a system of favours or invented news.

The renaissance in vinyl was sweet and somewhat encouraging, particularly if you're a 60 year-old white male who enjoys having old psychedelic or Madchester moments repackaged at him. Otherwise it's back to the old process of enjoying a random gig you've been invited to so much that you either buy a copy of the act's album after the show; or Google/Spotify them when you get back home later, still reeling from the otherworldly, transportive experience they'd taken you on a few hours before.

Put like that it might be the art that needs revitalising, rather than the model. Whether or not middle-aged-ish hacks should be writing about music or its delivery is a question I'll leave you to ponder on. Adam Ant might not (have) approve(d).

16

Conspiracy Theory or Counter-Discourse?

The degree to which someone is labelled a conspiracy theorist now entirely depends on the platform.

Ex-Mumford & Son Winston Marshall can talk to Laura Dodsworth about her new book on how the state weaponises fear amongst its citizens, but because it's a podcast on *Spectator TV*, it gets a pass. When Sonia Poulton or Richard Vobes do the same on their channels – to not dissimilar viewer numbers – they will be immediately rabbit-holed.

This isn't due to the content of whatever they're saying at any one time, rather than established positions of being pro and anti media messaging, whatever that message might be. It was family relationship-destroying during Brexit, then became gothic during the Covid lockdowns, as media narrative seemed to equate actual death. That is was really the old and already infirm statistically dying was by-the-by: you will be jabbed, and if you don't you will be unpersonned.

On the subject of health, should hospital managers

should be prosecuted for teen transitions; and on psychological well-being, should police superintendents be prosecuted for enabling false accusers? Increasing numbers think so. Neither Brexit, Covid, teen transitioning nor 'believe the victim' scandals were actually conspiracies: they all happened or are happening, but to go against the woke liberal democratic globalist party line was/is seen as the New Evil. Those arguing for patriotism, individualism, self-health determination or the innocent until proven guilty principle were tossed onto a bonfire of new heretics, cancelled, denied work, socially shunned, and 'othered' in any other way polite society could think of.

It was interesting how the media/public needed the confirmation of a corrupted justice system before celebrating Kevin Spacey and Andy Malkinson's exonerations. Evidence shouldn't have been hidden for twenty years in the Malkinson case, while he was in prison; and Spacey's trial should never have come to court, so flimsy was the testimony of his accusers. However it was only on this being confirmed by the courts did the papers all rush to condemn the broken systems that had allowed this to happen in the first place.

It's not just long-respected Hollywood stars such as Spacey that face the wrath of The Narrative: Jordan Peterson, Andrew Tate and Friedrich Nietzsche have also all been hung out to dry, dead or alive, over the years, for expressing their views on how masculinity should *be* in a still rampantly feminising West. The Matriarchy is here, while those in control claim the reverse, and continue to exercise anti-male processes in the family - and other - courts every day.

Parental Alienation is a growing concern, as fathers are alienated from their children by their ex-partners' threats, accusations and a multitude of other motivators - the money to be gained being one obvious one. Pop stars and folk devils are created and burned on a daily basis as the former speak their mind on any given hot topic, and the latter - who would essentially have been conventional criminals in the last century - are algorithmically crucified by a ravenous, bloodthirsty media culture that depends on their suffering for its survival.

Identity politics appears to be rapidly replacing party politics, as economic solutions and strategies are largely agreed upon in a post-economic ideological age, and cultural theorists root everything back to power dynamics between groups of people. The difference between diversity-sceptic and 'racist' has been eroded over the first decades of the twentieth century, as theorists decry the conventional 'colour-blindness' of the old woke establishment in favour of the divisionist critical race theory version of the new.

At least no one can say all the white men are winning everything any more, as awards shows are repeatedly called out for being 'so white' - making the whole entertainment industry a morass of lecturing message-fables, with a few fights and some gay sex thrown in for good measure. Executed prisoner maintaining innocence (and LA Crips founder) Stanley 'Tookie' Williams said his people were *'psychological captives to poverty'*, and that can increasingly be extended to everyone not considered in the elite Russell Group/Ivy League graduate media political class.

We are suffering a poverty of culture due to the stultifying, suffocating pressure of moralistic conscientiousness - a place where the conflation of creativity and morality doesn't necessarily do well. Historically nation states were and are based on what is now labelled racism, and the logical end of the current CRT hegemony is that decolonisation will end up with its proponents no longer using the English language: since language, according to the postmodernists at least, is power.

There is a moral equivalence between multinational corporations sponsoring the mutilation of children and Asian grooming gangs 'misunderstanding' British cultural values for years on end, but these descriptions result in an activists-against-minorities paradox that appears useful to no one. On the globalist front of all this, Klaus Schwab's Great Reset appears to be Dominic Cummings' new internationalist Blob versus the Individual, pitching woke globalism - hitherto referred to as Marxism by many - against the US right to bear arms (let alone the European Enlightenment tradition).

Some might say socialism by the back door, since individual states are likely to continue to democratically, if problematically, vote in their own best interests. In the UK traditionally supporting Labour and being 'cool' went hand in hand, but since Tony Blair's millennial back door revolution, no one wants to be seen siding with a mainstream party any more.

While singer Sinead O Connor did as much for the modernisation of Ireland as did U2's Bono, the late

DM-and-dungarees wearing singer's progressivism and attacks on the Catholic church set her out as very much a woman of her times, though angry and troubled unto death. The abuse once rife in the Catholic church was labelled conspiracy talk for years before too much evidence exposed it as largely true. Why are the untimely causes of famous peoples' passing not mentioned since Robin Williams' suicide in the 2010s? Presumably the public can't be trusted to handle the truth.

But Catholicism is relatively ancient. The new conspiracies revolve around new progressive forms being allied to old divisions, with movements live Black Lives Matter, #MeToo, MAGA or European populism serving as useful signifiers of newly individuated resistance. Much of the mainstream media is implicated in this having come to pass, while its working model is still based on fear. Now however the resistance voices are equally loud due to the prevalence of the independent internet: so at what point will the conspiracy theories return to being what they always actually were – evidence of a democratically essential counter-discourse?

17

Men and Masculinity

Men and masculinity have been under attack across the West for much of the 21st century so far. The hundred year-long struggle for equal rights under feminism culminated in the Equality Act 2010 in the UK, when the war was in essence won. Niggles such as intra-cultural pay gaps remained, let alone traditional and religious attitudes to gendered roles, but by and large equity had been achieved.

Following contemporaneous Title IX sex laws being fully industrialised in the US punishing sexual discrimination, harassment and assault on campuses - and beyond - #MeToo arrived around 2017 to decimate the entertainment industry, for better or worse. From tiny, positive acorns, massive mixed-blessing oaks can grow, and a 1970s version of radical feminism – *'all men are rapists, thus must be minimised'* – became amplified by the binary-attraction model of internet algorithms.

While this sort of thinking had been hitherto relegated to bitter eccentrics in unloved corners of academia, suddenly it was grafted into the souls of attractive young heteronormative types, ready to tweet. The myth that women were still ignored in a patriarchal society seemed hard to give up, even as the matriarchy took over every lever of power from publishing to government, sliding messaging out anonymously through social media departments.

In poll after poll feminism as an identity to be supported or with which to identify could not surpass 10% prevalence with the public, while domestic violence and sexual assault statistics were re-written in ways favourable to the RadFem cause. High profile men such as Jimmy Saville, Rolf Harris, Harvey Weinstein, Woody Allen and Jeffrey Epstein found themselves posthumously cancelled or in prison due to sexual allegations various. Others, such as Cliff Richard, Paul Gambaccini and Kevin Spacey found themselves falsely accused but facing massive legal hurdles (and no small degree of post-traumatic stress disorder).

The younger the man in question as time went on, the more problematic the allegations, as the contexts became greyer and greyer. Whether it was law student Liam Allan being falsely accused of rape by a disgruntled ex girlfriend, goth rocker Marilyn Manson facing down numerous lawsuits, or both ex-US president Donald Trump being found liable for sexual assault and incumbent Joe Biden – he who had signed off the Title IX-enacting *'Dear Colleague'* letter in the first place - being accused of 'digital penetration', the gloves were off.

The more public mouthpieces such as family court barrister Charlotte Proudman, academic Jess Taylor and MP Jess Philips were facilitated in increasingly shrill discourse, the more gerrymandered the statistics became. Non-politicised figures such as Cheryl Thomas KC, Canadian academic Janice Fiamengo and Australian journalist Bettina Arndt calmly pointed out the reality behind the headlines, thus enraging the legions of hitherto dormant power-fembots lined up ready to slay rhetorical across the algorithms.

Men's disquiet with what felt like completely one-sided sexual politic propaganda was growing – and their concern became increasingly echoed in more traditionally-minded women. This traditional-mindedness simply meant those who believed that men and women were at their best when working together, rather than trying to destroy each other in an intersectional, indoctrinated power game.

Andrew Tate brandished his pecs, Masarati, cigars and aviators, and amassed an army of disenfranchised young men (and women) before being put under house arrest in Romania on suspicion of rape and human trafficking. Saifullah Khan took Yale University to court for improperly carried out sexual assault investigations, claiming false allegations had stolen his future - and won. Comedian and neo-political activist Russell Brand had his communication channels cancelled due to coordinated allegations made against his sexual past via *Channel 4* and *The Sunday Times*, a decade after a similar trick had been successfully pulled on WikiLeaker Julian Assange (whose extradition woes rumbled on).

Men's rights activists, often portrayed as far-rightists by the power-feminists, have generally done their best to look after the state of increasingly done-down men and boys, as mothers found their husbands and sons falsely accused and fathers forbidden from seeing their children by an almost completely captured family court system. Paul Elam of the XY Crew in the US, Mike Buchanan of the Justice for Men and Boys organisation in the UK try to sneak out their exasperated message via (occasionally) Piers Morgan on Talk TV or YouTube personality Pearl Davis, but the discourse remains decidedly 'counter'.

While legal dominance and power-feminists capitalise on every inter-personal sexual-political news story, online MRAs will repeatedly point to white working class boys being the worst performing demographic in society, turning to Incel (involuntary celibate) culture as a result. MGTOW *(Men Going Their Own Way)* has become a movement in itself: including Passport Bros, who are western males travelling abroad to look for or to be with women who aren't preoccupied with power dynamics, and are more interested in a peaceful, cooperative, unindoctrinated life.

While it often feels like third and/or fourth wave feminism is in a permanent state of arrested development adolescence, collective masculinity has of late been tiring of being the patient adult in the room, being quietly tolerant as the disruptive delinquent smashes up the kitchen. It's fully understandable that a new form of post-MeToo male assertion is possible: needing no hate, resentment or even conflict.

Many of those already in long-term relationships are no doubt happy with their situations, but those terrified of the new pitfalls of modern dating and relationships would be forgiven for turning their backs on the whole shebang. This doesn't mean turning gay, or becoming addicted to porn; it means focussing creative and adventurous energy on other things, about reassessing aims beyond the indoctrination to nest: how can anyone nest when it's so full of risk, and mostly for men? If the feminists wanted the end of heteronormativity, they might have almost achieved it.

A male view on the act of sex has been entirely ignored in culture - when that culture isn't too squeamish to even go there. Emasculated, feminised gyneocentrism is the only sexual conversation in town, even though any mutually satisfactory experience takes two to meaningfully tango. In moving forward from the current chronically biased situation, a Minister for Men in the UK – since there has been a Minister for Women since 1997 – would be a useful voice in UK Parliament. Beyond that, a post-#MeToo Men's Amnesty could be possible, where males are open about what they want, what they deserve, and what is fair, expressed without fear or favour, and also without having to be looked at through the prism of feminism.

The term 'toxic masculinity' needs to be expunged from common discourse in the way that have been racial slurs, and identity theories as they are currently weaponised need to be recognised as the psychological abuse they are. The progressive left shibboleth *'have fewer babies to save your independence and the Earth'* could be being achieved by stealth through this 'men walking away', quietly and surreptitiously, as the psycho-spiritual pressure increases, and so the ideological replacement strategy continues. This replacement theory is a political tactic of removing powerful people by whatever means, and replacing them with approved, on-message characters.

Beyond conflict there must be resolution, even when that conflict becomes intra-national rather than international. Whether that happens by males setting aside romantic or domestic ambitions while aiming their unique energies in less risky directions should be less a matter of bleak desperation rather than one of enlightened choice.

18

Critical Identity Theory and Higher Arts Education – A Mini-Memoir

In the late 1990s I started a degree in Fine Art at the then Surrey Institute of Art and Design University College, subsequently renamed the University for the Creative Arts in the seemingly inevitable process of art school corporatisation.

While I restlessly genre-hopped, one of my co-undergraduates was multimedia artist Steve Cutts – later animator of the *'Man'* short films. While we worked in our studio spaces, a handful of tutors, many with Masters degrees, most pursuing PhD's, would occasionally hover around. In fairness art is, or should be, totally subjective, so it can be delicate for an overseer to know when to intervene.

In personal and group tutorials, Steve would be lost for words in trying to describe why an installation consisted of a reassembled crashed yellow Ferrari, with a bloodied, papier-mache 'Gary' hanging out of it, grinning at the wheel. Tripping from decorative abstracts to emotionally descriptive video art, I was also at a loss as to saying how I was critiquing culture, but remember feeling a pressure to describe a series of pure abstracts as some sort of comment on Tony Blair's 'Third Way' policies.

To justify the £9000 per year tuition fees Blair had suddenly brought in after coming to power, and in a desperate attempt to rationalise the amorphous, right-brain process of genuine creativity, our far Left-leaning tutors felt a compulsion to look for political or identity meaning in everything. We were essentially alone amongst dozens of women in our year in resisting the pressure to apply identitarianism to our work, as otherwise it would presumably be marked down or implicitly dismissed as 'mere trinkets'. Still, some artists are less susceptible to emotional blackmail than others, so we ploughed on regardless, eventually getting our degrees.

But what were we now in debt *for?* Essentially for being granted three years out to explore our creative spirits; but the apparent price for this, and the 'networking' necessary for future opportunities, was an open-armed embrace of what would in the future come to be called 'woke' critical theories. In the pub following group tutorials, Steve would regularly wonder why all his other co-sculptors would endlessly make work about 'identity', often while the work more looked like piles of tidily arranged cushions etc. It was as if art that didn't somehow comment on the social issues in identity politics, it was somehow of a lesser standard.

It was only a dogged belief in our own internal visual language that pulled us through, with some degree of artistic self-respect intact. Subsequently we went on to become variously successful - if such a value can be applied to art, at least financially - as Steve animated videos for Moby and accrued millions of YouTube views for his Manimations.

The main finding was that the people who were pressurised into seeing their art as being correspondent with socio-political issues tended to seem rather depressed about what they were doing, whereas those who followed their own inner compass only increased their passion for their own production (albeit through adversity).

So yes, if you had - or have - the skills you may become some sort of a visual artist; but if you don't internalise and then endlessly reference identity political bias, you were – and presumably still are - seen as irrelevant.

19

The Rocky Horror Picture Show & the Great Trans Debate

For many people, the ire with which the Trans Wars are fought is quite mystifying. This is because, far from what might some call transphobia, there is something much more like conflict bemusement.

For those born in or experiencing later than the 1970s, the whole personal identity question has been weaponised beyond all recognition of those who fought the original struggles for equal societal rights. One group of these would be what once would have been called transsexuals, sometimes identifying as transvestites, and some even claiming to come from Transylvania.

Only latterly discovered to be somewhere around Romania, in the early 70s it was literally a product of the (far earlier) Bram Stoker's imagination, as actor/writer Richard O'Brien juxtaposed the late Victorian era with the glamorous cross-dressing scene of twentieth century underground culture. The thing is, then and now, was that The Rocky Horror Picture Show was a riotous, anarchic, happy romp of a time, that was life-affirming in celluloid and long-lasting on stage, touring all over to this day.

The spectacularly charismatic Tim Curry as *Dr Frank-n-Furter*, Susan Sarandon as the innocent Janet and a biker cameo by Meat Loaf demonstrated the broad post-hippy liberal consensus that characterised the time, when Janet's husband Brad and *the Narrator* were on the repressed right, but Frank and O' Brien's vampiric Riff-Raff were (probably) of the left. The Transexuals' Castle became a seventies style Gatsby mansion, where the post-war strictures of 50s America were decanted into the golden glitter-pants era of Rocky – a tanned, muscled nu-Frankenstein's monster, mute but handsome, signifying the coming youth.

Fast forward through fifty years, and every equal rights movement from racial equality to stammerers rights had gained parity via the protected characteristics laws of the early twentieth century. Over this process, and largely due to the democratic right of multi-lateral freedom of expression amplified by the internet, those still minority positions had been further balkanised and often re-marginalised.

This is because laws are passed and rights are enshrined, but opinions often don't budge: many people feel that men are men, women are women, and that's that. This can come from reasons of religion, upbringing or an understanding of nature that doesn't exactly correspond with the progressives' train-tracks. Democratic society, while protecting the rights of everyone so long as they're not harming anyone else, hasn't yet reconciled the majority to the principle of self-identification.

While Ru Paul or Frank-n-Furter could flamboyantly entertain to their hearts' content, Midwest America or home counties England will only look on and possibly celebrate their own tolerance, not those peoples' rights to identify as whatever or whomever they wish. This comes less from an ingrained religious feeling, since Christianity for one has been so winnowed down, as from a suspicion that it's all a phase, since the majority don't choose to do this, any more than not everyone could paint like Picasso, so why should they? They could try, and move through fashions, but never really get there according to the messages received by the televisions in the corners of most living rooms.

Western mainstream culture, which has more in common with that of Russia, China and various Islamic republics than most in the west would like to admit, is not convinced by what it sees as identity entertainment, let alone sexual behaviours not 'Of the book' (in Jordan Peterson's terminology). When it's a man pretending to be a woman, a la Danny La Rue, Zeki Muren or Julian Clary, the country will pat itself on the back and congratulate itself on how open minded it is. The difference is in the fact that Rocky Horror, in the UK at least, is experienced as a multi-directional, bone-deep art, including show tunes, a joyful feeling of sensuality, scintillating rock and roll and some electrifyingly ramshackle performances.

Mainstream acting can handle other peoples' sexual choices on a stage. It was pretending to be able to tolerate it as a genuine lifestyle choice for many years, while traditional mindsets pretended to tolerantly approve. After so many years and so much cultural attrition, the question *'Approve of what exactly?'* is a reasonable one.

20

With New Eyes: Art and Academia in the 21st Century

An oft-heard mumble emanating from many observers of art in galleries across the modern world goes along the lines of: *"My five year old could have done that"* - demonstrating the challenges behind the mainstream reception of Challenging Art. The left-brain dominated system in which we live demands recognisable images, and this was the character of most western art for centuries before the invention of photography and its freeing technology.

Mid-twentieth century American critic Clement Greenberg went on to assert the primacy of 'the artist' in the appreciation of art, and encouraging the ethos of *'art for art's sake'*. This elevated the moment of creation over the desire in the viewer for verisimilitude, and allowed for anything the artist made to be treated with a certain near-religious regard. As minimalism and conceptualism forced art down a cerebral rabbit-hole, Pop Art and postmodernism opened up infinite new possibilities.

The former involved the highbrow celebration of celebrity culture, while the latter said that anything could now be art, whether new, combined with the traditional or anything else. Art theorists were desperate to stay relevant, so postmodern art eventually spread to postmodern science, involving all iterations of incipient transhumanism, from clones to AI. It was just waiting for technology to catch up - which going into the 21st century, it did.

All this postmodern chaos occurred alongside the democratisation of information known as the Internet: news becoming devalued, and a societal feeling of creeping unreality increasingly presented as reality. Traditional socialist ideas were still around but gradually developed into a more mannered 'kindness' as opposed to the gnarlier ownership-of-the-means-of-production of yore. The rioting hippies of 1968 were now University Vice-Chancellors and Deans - having privately never lost their Marxist zeal - and were ensuring all hires to the Western academy were either hard-left or at least left-leaning.

The power of group-think and lack of enthusiasm for having generous pay packets circumscribed led to the adoption of leftist social progressivism as the universal mentality of higher education: Nietzsche's spiritual individualism be damned. This led to visiting speakers being cancelled when the radicalised students - who were increasingly responsible for those pay packets - organised online petitions to have those marginal speakers whose published views they found so anti their values.

It was understood by Oxford Chancellor Chris Patten, for one, that this kind of intellectual cherry-picking would be disastrous for the sort of universally holistic education for which Oxbridge was famed, and which was the very point of the Enlightenment tradition. Returning openness to education and the arts across the Anglosphere became a talisman of right-leaning media, inverting the century-old truism of rebellion coming from the left.

'I won't define you if you don't define me' became the mantra of inclusivity, diversity and equity, the New Labour-spawned religion of millennial ubiquity, leading to a sort of moral relativism that contained a built-in, potentially culturally suicidal race-to-the-bottom. Not judging others for anything that they were or did led to an erosion of critical faculty - and when it was attempted by the independent-minded or the bold, was met with cries of *'Fascist!'*

The marginalisation of the natural man, always hovering, as long-held understandings of humankind based on the fact that human beings are a part of nature were defenestrated as either 'unkind', heteronormative, or otherwise unacceptably traditional. The fact that just as many men as women agreed with these understandings, of all races - and much more so in non-white areas - was deemed irrelevant to the progressive elite, who now had a firm stranglehold on education, state culture and the media. A drop of water is a universe to an atom, and a marginal fightback was underway – but this would generally be framed as conservative, backwards, or 'far right'.

An explosion in post-woke, post-covid decadent art was hungrily anticipated, but while the new creed of identitarianism was in force across western culture, expressions of instinct were immediately cancelled on X or called out due to potential for 'reputational damage'. Still the new tech lords of Silicon Valley and beyond were rolling in the numbers, with a few hard-heads such as Elon Musk trying to hang onto a slipping conception of naturalism.

Whether anybody would be allowed to read this into their perceptions of handmade abstract art - a subjectified way of seeing dismissed and disposed of as 'degenerate' by the actual Nazis - remained to be seen.

21

Swift On Wax - Identity Politics and The Music Industry

The Brit Awards recently had no women in their best artist category since opting for gender neutral categories last year (when Adele controversially celebrated the fact that she was proud to be a woman) - since the bestsellers were all men. Concurrently, the traditionally enthusiasts' favourite – vinyl - has overtaken CDs as the most bought physical medium, with Taylor Swift leading sales.

What *does* it say that all the best sellers were men? Does it say anything, or is it just how the cookie crumbled at the time? British non-binary crooner Sam Smith said *"[The Brits] just have to celebrate everyone because this is not just about artists getting awards. Awards are for kids watching on TV, thinking, 'I can make music like this'"*.

Why is it important that young music or film lovers see themselves singing back at themselves from the silver screen? Isn't the confected factory of the dream machine about creating new alternative realities into which to step, rather than constantly trying to 'own' that place?

Would it be better to have gender segregation to

celebrate lesser-selling albums just because they're by women? Historically vinyl has been a super-male form, like gaming and old-school PCs. Gradually the tech overlords have marketed it to be first useful, then cool, then indispensable. The pushing of sexual equality in the media is as much a financial concern as a humanistic one, and it was only a matter of time before the multifaceted rights brigade were going to putsch for their representation too.

Eight-track cartidges in the 1960s were superseded by vinyl in the 70s; cassettes in the 80s were replaced by CDs in the 1990s; reaching a kind of maximum price, maximum exposure watershed in around 1997. Post Blair/Diana/Clinton, Napster took over, music became liquid, and David Bowie's prediction of music being as available as water from a tap gradually became true.

Now, the medium has become more interesting and important than the cultural movements from the physical 20th century, as the listeners opt for the ease of itunes and Spotify, and the eras of identifying as mods, rockers, punks and goths morphed into identifying as gay, anti-racist, non-binary, vaccine-skeptic etc.

That nagging sense of wanting something physical of the artist remains though, particularly when the artist is as iconic as someone like Taylor Swift (or Led Zeppelin for that matter). So the black vinyl album, that exquisitely minimal memorium in wax, enjoys a resurgence in buyer's choice, the market deciding which format it best likes to hear its heroines and heroes. And that choice is circular (insert pronouns at will).

The Internet had both a destructive and renewing effect on the music industry, roughly as the centuries turned. The Net was also quickly seen by activists as a useful tool towards unmandated social change, leading to the Obama election, Occupy, the Arab Spring, #MeToo, Black Lives Matter and many more. This well-meaning social change has led to other areas dangerous to artistic free expression, such as cancel culture, groupthink and progressive hegemony in the arts and education.

These developments have led to a strange situation where the traditional Right have become the rebels, signalling issues like the excesses of trans activism or the silenced howl of protest that is the post-feminist phenomenon of Incel culture. Pretending that the impressive sales of Adele and Swift aren't connected to these intersectional social movements would be disengenuous, and is another area in which the media story has become more important than the content of the work presented.

22

The Online Court of New Moral Behaviour

The term 'Woke' emerged from the campuses of some North American universities in the mid to late 2010's, well before the Black Lives Matter protests. The word's grammatical mangling of the meaning of 'awake' explains a great deal of the success of its being hijacked by the (alt) right, containing as it does a degree of unspoken outrage that the progressives should define the narrative, let alone the grammar, in this way.

During the 1990's UK university libraries were stacked full of books on race and gender critical theory, whether their main constituency were students of maths, economics or graphic design. The hippies and punks of the 60's and 70's social revolutions had worked out that they wouldn't shift traditional attitudes by elections alone, so would have to play the long game, the slow attrition of multilateral change, effected along the way by getting into power at the top of media, justice and education organisations.

Identitarianism soon followed, and its progress was akin to lava down a volcano's slopes, slowly preparing to engulf the manifold dwellings in its path. Criticisms were met with instant, knee-jerk counter claims of dinosaur, gammon, pale male and stale, Karen, fascist, sexual assault apologist, conspiracy theorist and anything else pithy and difficult to argue with without looking like the label. These new identity politics were classical rhetoric deployed with death threats, with the main intention to be to stay at the top of the headlines, because from there, cultural conversation and the state money that goes with it were guaranteed.

The largely white, ageing, middle-class, liberal-minded protesters of Extinction Rebellion often mumble to camera, while an emergency worker tries to jimmy the glue from their hands, that their actions may be unpopular, but *'at least it got the media's attention'*. This social justice updating of the 'there's no such thing as bad publicity' principle ignores the fact that any government needs the enthusiastic consent of the majority of the people to effect a change as radical as zero-carboning an entire country.

As it is, this Waitrose faction of the culture wars are simply setting back the zero-carbon plan by decades, at least in terms of hearts and minds. Those once from the left, but no longer of the left have been forced into that position by progressive attacks on free speech, again emanating from the campuses via Twitter, and immediately weaponised by the other side.

'Traditional' feminists and transgender activists, once on the same team, now bite lumps out of each other online, in an absolute gift to the traditionalists. The feminists now look Jurassic in their own way, while the transgender lobby are full of the vim of their every identity-challenging wish being granted.

Online, and increasingly on the streets, the Pride festival and programmes like Ru-Paul's Drag Race and Naked Attraction are praised with an unquestioning devotion akin to the Sermon from the Mount, while a Peter Hitchens article or Laurence Fox broadcast are as vilified as the utterings of evil emanating from Linda Blair's mouth in The Exorcist.

This (weaponised) woke identitarianism isn't a figment of the imagination of a small cabal of indigenous Brits; it's a brilliant media invention, opportunised as a gift when that industry has been balkanised almost into irrelevance by the seemingly unstoppable march towards Internet singularity.

Evidence hasn't been necessary to convict for certain categories of case in UK law since 2003, when ex-barristers Tony and Cherie Blair used the New Labour majority to introduce the Balance of Probabilities test for juries to follow, essentially ending the centuries-long Innocent Until Proven Guilty principle. They had facilitated the 'No smoke without fire' instinct, in order to move the vast majority of grey area cases into the human dustbin of the modern prison, just as the Internet was starting to become endemic, and embedded.

Twitter, Facebook et al had become Elon Musk's new town square, and anyone who wanted to be part of the cultural conversation had better be on it, brown paper bag in hand. Problem was, you needed to be in-group. If you believed in the masculine, dynamic, genetics-first, no nonsense, red-meat view of life, you were a neo-fascist who voted for the UK to leave the European Union, and probably a royalist. If you believed in a feminine, consensus-finding, nurturing, compassionate, out-group hating view, you were now part of the New Establishment.

To question anyone's self-identifying to this group was seen as patronising 'mansplaining', and would lead to reasonably polite if also condescending imprecations to *'check your thinking'*. If you looked like you identified as a two-sided spirit penguin going forward, that was your business; but it did also once lead to Piers Morgan auto-combusting live on national television.

People have been angsting about trial by media for a long time now, since the advent of TV, then the rampant tabloidisation of the newspaper business in the 1980s. Trial by social media is very different however. It is instant, leaves no time for reflection or nuance, and its business model is based - much like in the legacy media - on conflict, and having that keeping us tuning in.

The competition and bullying is stressing the kids, the in-group obligation and professional entreaties to *'post that, it's great'* is distracting the adults from the depth of integrity required to live an enriched life. Jean Baudrillard's hyperreal has become the everyday, we never log out and 5G (or wherever we are now) has made it all smoother than ever. Is a suspect more guilty after they had the thought to pull the trigger, whether they were draped in a rainbow flag, after they pulled it, or when they tapped *'Post'*?

23

Punching Up with Dr Shola (and friends)

The new industry of 'race-baiting' on mainstream television

Dr Shola Mos-Shogbamimu, Yasmin Alibhai-Brown and Adjoa Andoh comprise a wider phalanx of critical theory that is regularly invited onto mainstream television channels. There is little these women say that doesn't include an attack on British history or the social status of ethnic minority people in the UK.

While freedom of speech is vital, they regularly push that envelope with attacks that in the not so distant past would have been described as treasonous. Shola Mos essentially celebrated Queen Elizabeth II's death, Alibhai-Brown regularly bemoans the racism that she helps instigate, and Andoh can't get through an interview without bringing up black representation in every industry going, regardless of merit.

Critical theory insists on power dynamics between people on every level, while ignoring factors such as the soul, the spirit, genetic tendencies or bloodlines. This pseudo hard-headed approach might seem cool in the student common room, but there are more things in heaven and earth than are dreamt of in your philosophy, David Olusoga. It's almost as if a hundred CRT lecturers had groomed a thousand media students as to using industry DEI policies in how to get on screen, and then set to prove Jim Morrison's quote 'Whoever controls the media, controls the mind'.

In a competitive media environment increasingly reliant on impact and clicks for advertising income, the programme producers won't be bothered about the social division caused by their steady attacks on the tacit UK social code. While the media has always been amoral when it is working properly – that is part of its remit – there are also campaigning editors and channels at work, with cultural-political agendas of their own.

System-wide diversity, equity and inclusion policies have been weaponised as a useful tool in attacking societally embedded ways of life, resulting in a gradual chipping away at the depth of culture. The critical race theory being taught in universities for the last half a century has been rocket-boosted by a now largely subjective social media landscape. Where once one studio would broadcast to millions, now one individual just needs to broadcast to their followers in as catchy and impactful a way as to emotionally affect others outside it enough to share. This has become utilizing hive-mind groupthink as intra-national propaganda.

It didn't take long for the truism 'bad news sells' to become understood by a new, often untrained media class to constantly stoke outrage in 'the other', to essentially make a career out of winding others up. Black thinkers such as Thomas Sowell and Morgan Freeman have tried to encourage other members of their community to think about the present and future rather than the distant past, but politicised critical theorists insist on tormenting the living for the ancient trading standards of Empires. That the ancient Assyrian empire (soon followed by the Egyptian) invented what is now known as slavery is usually ignored, as is the fact that the British empire was the first to campaign to end it.

High Priestess of Hollywood CRT-in-exile Meghan Markle, having already brought her influence into the Royal Family, geographically exited it as quickly as possible - taking her Lord of the Woke husband Harry back to the slums of Montecito with her. Meghan and Oprah Winfrey's brand of 'be kind' virtue-signalling has had a convenient and emasculating effect on the critical race diaspora, allowing reverse-progress for a century of human rights cooperation to flourish.

This is achieved by the spannering of ready media-trained tears and threats of suicide via willing PR strategists into press releases, thereby further stigmatizing an individual's ultimate choice and degrading the pain of the genuinely suicide-bereaved everywhere. Weaponising the impossible-to-verify is a postmodern hallmark of this sort of media training. This sort of empathy sells. We're often told that anti-white rhetoric on television is acceptable as it's 'punching up' - i.e. the socially disadvantaged attacking the privileged - but the reality is that Dr Shola with her academic credentia and media fees is actually punching down onto the white working class boys, girls and other watching her on daytime TV.

Yes it's a blatant grift, and yes they probably do all receive various levels of online threats, but these are the wages of winding up the majority of people who are inadvertently paying your wages, through the producers endlessly booking this sort of societally destructive visual clickbait. Be kind, educate yourself, do better, etc.

24

Trans, Dada and Individualism in Art

Two young women recently threw some paint over one of Vincent Van Gogh's series of Sunflowers paintings. Thankfully it was protected by glass, but these adorable scamps had made their point. It didn't matter how hallowed the work of art, making their point and getting their t-shirts into the headlines just for one day was more important than the mass derision it would cause, and how in their echo chambered cultural vandalism minds, this attention was somehow worth it.

As if the adults didn't realise oil had become something of an issue. As if most of them had time or resources to do anything about it other than the recycling most have been doing for years. It was enraging to a white, indigenous, reasonably educated heterosexual male. To some others too, by all accounts.

There is however a strong tradition of active protest as art, going back to the Dada movement of the early twentieth century, where cultural hooliganism was seen as some sort of intellectual offshoot of conscientiously objecting to the mass slaughter of one world war, with the spectre of another possibly looming. Revolutionary Marxists, setting up in Moscow, were bolting down the USSR and declaring most bourgeois western art decadent – a trick later also employed by the far right.

Chess-playing professional Frenchman Marcel Duchamp invented the ongoing irritation of conceptual art by presenting a urinal as a 'ready-made' sculpture, Salvador Dali was beginning to celebrate the absurd, and anything counter-cultural was seen as fair game. Dada was very much the conceptual precursor to Monty Python's Flying Circus in the later television age, but with more extra-marital sex, snuff and possibly opium (for those who could afford it).

The transvestitism of the Berlin scene was a fringe entertainment of this counter-culture, a sexualised version of the more bawdy music hall turns all across Britain. An eyeliner pencil can trace a line from the late 19th century decadence of Oscar Wilde to the inter-war expat adventures of Christopher Isherwood's Berlin, and on to the Rocky Horror Picture Show glam of the early to mid-1970s.

It was pretence, it was the other, it was relaxation... but it wasn't biology. The structuralism of becoming *'the other'* couldn't be chosen on a cellular level. That was because we were in a time of exploratory modernism. Come postmodernism – often thought of around 1980 – and thinkers such as Baudrillard, Barthes and Lyotard were trying to pinpoint what the next century would bring. Whether any of them predicted a redesigning of nature-given sexuality by the power of individual choice is unlikely.

Biology first, social engineering second would appear to follow a certain natural sense – but sense is apparently a product of the historical patriarchy, as ripe to be demonised and defenestrated as slavery, colonialism or antisemitism. It's politically incoherent too, but no one I know started that: it's the chaotic redesigning of liberal values by each dissatisfied generation, whittling down received science as they go.

Many who were 'from' the left gradually became no longer 'of' the left, as their carnival of human rights left those of some – notably natural born women – stranded out in the new apolitical cold. Many bullied at school defined themselves as living lives of modern adversity due to those they saw as the heteronormative fascists around them.

This new joy of disunity seemed to be celebrated in academia, as Oxford, Cambridge and Harvard championed their staff - and increasingly students - in self-identifying as whatever they chose, as academic objectivity was thrown onto the bonfire of old thought, and the youthful chaos of the mixed heritage, pangender-fluid green vegan uberwimmin (and their gentleman sympathisers) asserted their post-feminist dominance.

Societal sympathy for the youth was doing its best to look beyond rationality to the rights of the individual to help them lead their best lives, but found themselves having to refer to once chippy, aggy, unattractive old men as 'they' when they were a singular being, in an ongoing mauling of the hitherto super-flexible English language. Anything was better than dead-naming someone by accident when your livelihood and professional reputation was on the line.

Many didn't even get the madness memo – how could it be written? - meaning that they could stumble over the social cliff by accident, drunk, bug-eyed and spinning on the lithium rush of post-structuralist queer theory. The disciplinarian of old had no cane any more, as the The Skewer satirised the malleability of message on newly funky Radio 4 and the *'Believe the Victims'* policy upturned the principle of innocent until proven guilty in the courts; a dark new development of the primacy of individual (female) rights.

These two kinds of postmodernism – hyper-satire and self-identification – were beginning to define the culture in general, destroying humour and other agreed terms in a mass scorched earth policy, emanating from Silicon Valley and Harvard, searing across the Atlantic and onto the BBC.

Duchamp and Dada's sketches from the culture wars had been drafted between the world wars of the twentieth century, the British art school tradition had been quietly pushing this strange envelope since the 1960s, and by the early decades of the new millennium its messages had permeated how developing, plastic-brained people saw themselves.

Once drawing a moustache of a photocopy of the Mona Lisa might have been enough to scratch a revolutionary British itch: now it takes a full tin of paint, with an iphone in hand to livestream it.

25

The Bonfire of Agreed Terms

Lonely hearts ad: '*Middle-aged person seeking someone with zero aspirations who is happy to simply enjoy the moment, because all unhappiness seems to spring from unmet expectations*'.

Men are from Mars and Women are from Venus, as a bestselling book once had it, maintaining that the binaries of male and female patterned brains were a biological reality (even if the book put it in more psycho-spiritual terms). Women feel better through talking about what's on their minds and cry readily, sometimes enjoying the cathartic reaction, and often feeling affirmation from any sympathy elicited. Anthropologically speaking, they and their offspring are likely to do better if their tribe likes them and wants to look after their interests.

Men prefer to work these things out on their own, usually having a much higher bar for allowing tears, but when they do talk about serious problems it's generally because all other avenues to a solution have failed. Both strategies have their upsides and downsides, but each sex seems to have difficulty truly understanding the position of the other, leading to a seemingly endless war of attrition.

This can go to the more toxic area of false or spurious allegations, borne of the fact that the different sexes see 'Abuse' in different ways. False allegations can be seen as a form of psychological abuse. Globally, women are statistically more likely to engage in psychological abuse than men: governments need to enact and enforce laws designed to impose sanctions on false accusers, whatever the gender, 'dead-naming' be damned.

In his provocatively titled book The Ugly Feminist, Mike Buchanan of the UK's Justice for Men and Boys Party discusses different-pattern brains: how Margaret Thatcher thought strategically and pragmatically for example, male-pattern traits in a female psysiology. Increasingly in culture (if not ruling politics) politicians such as Sir Keir Starmer integrate subjective feelings into their policies in order not to alienate the female vote. The fact that the Conservative Party has had three prime ministers in its history whereas the Labour party - for all its progressive values - has had none, speaks volumes in itself.

The Bonfire of Agreed Terms is affecting the cultural politics of the West on a daily basis, as the claim that the patriarchy is responsible for those implacable structures persists, and pliant men are being co-opted into believing that a gender-feminist ruled world, achieved by positive discrimination in elections, is a valid idea in terms of some by now catastrophically spurious resetting of the gender pendulum.

It's increasingly as if there are two English languages, one for received traditional values and another for international 'progressives'; and while the letters are the same, the hitherto agreed terms of not punching down, criticism having a place alongside empathy and the very nature of He/She binaries have all been consumed and spat out by the mincer of the extremes of postmodern cultural thinking.

The English language thrives as the international language by mutual consent, but race and gender critical theory have pulled this apart and are obsessed with resetting narratives in the media – as that is where changing minds truly lies, rather than at the ballot box. The biological male meanwhile lurks in the background like the Holocaust behind Germany, obliged to feel guilt for the past actions of his supposed ancestral power-mongers - even when (or particularly because of the fact that) everyone of his nation ultimately benefited, as that was the driving force of those times, disobeyed on pain of death.

Lives of accidental violence (physical or psychological) permeate relationships formed in the 21st century, already cauterised by a myriad critical theory discourses as they are. This isn't restricted to the university educated – though it's most eloquently expressed there – but trickles down through TV programmes and magazines into the pubs, clubs and salons, forcing ideological wedges between hitherto happily rubbing-along couples.

It is held by gender activists that the majority of

intimate partner violence or abuse is perpetrated by the male against the female, but the reality is that females have been steadily encouraged to report their concerns more over a number of decades. Very violent, salacious stories make it to the papers, and can be quite regular, even when the sample group contains millions of people.

Thus the 'toxic relationship', often gone terribly wrong, between two people becomes a poster case for what's happening in every other couples' lives. The human element of these stories, as with soap operas, is compelling, and real facts and stats become secondary to objectivity in a cultural landscape where clicks and hits rule in terms of site, paper, editor and writer getting paid.

The much-more-equal-than-widely-reported nature of domestic violence, tragic as these stories often are, becomes thence instantly weaponised by those with an interest in prizing the victimhood of one gender over another. The demonisation of men through the campaigning editors of the mainstream media is continued through the prejudicial decisions of family courts throughout the West - and an increasingly endemic parental alienation is the result.

Literally no-one wins from this situation, toxic points which often could have been countered by genuinely objective Conflict Resolution long beforehand. But no, the 'Believe the Victims' mantra must be obeyed, even when the man is late to to party in asserting who the victim actually is (see: Johnny Depp, and thousands of lesser-known others).

Our tentatively optimistic Romeo or Juliet, planning

nervously on placing their Lonely Heart ad might want to check the pronouns of their prospective date: if they are declared, as they're increasingly required to be, it's more than likely that they've already drunk the Kool-Aid of the Woke Brigade, and that all hopes of natural sense are lost. (Or there's always a Pre-Nup agreement if things go well - even if Non-Disclosure Agreements are increasingly and counter-intuitively being disclosed by a moralising activist culture, keen on witch-huntery.)

Might be best to stay in and watch Netflix on your own, safe in the knowledge that your sense of your own biology - and responsibility for it - is at least your own. For now.

26

In Your Own Time: Disconnected

As with the subjects of incest, paedophilia and cannibalism, suicide has occasionally had its place in the sun as 'society's last taboo'. Indeed there are daily media stories which use the threat of suicide as a sort of tool for emotional blackmail, standing as it does as an unquestionable totem of mental health last resort.

And it certainly is that: life is a mystery given, and it seems counter-intuitive at least to take it away. This extends to the question of whether suicide is a moral choice, as held by the Abrahamic religions of Judaism, Christianity and Islam, punishable as sin; or if it is a humanistic one, as held out by 20th century existentialist philosophers such as Camus, Sartre or Kierkegaard. New South African documentary film Disconnected artfully broaches some of these questions, taking in as it does as talking heads a rabbi, a bi-polar patient, mental health professionals and grieving mothers.

To choose the time of answering The Big Question, for the actor to leave the stage before the curtain comes down, seems intuitively like a mental health issue: but research shows that around 50% of suicide cases have no such history. Included is the story of a happy, rounded, outwardly balanced, middle-class mother who got into heavy debt, so simply went to her garage one morning, started her car, attached a hosepipe and let things take their course.

Without needing to reference high profile historical cases such as the poet, writer and Mrs Ted Hughes (who lost not one wife but two to suicide) Sylvia Plath, Nirvana frontman Kurt Cobain or comic genius Robin Williams, it's clear that they who truly suffer are those left behind. In the cases of these famous figures, their families extend to the millions who loved them for their work. But, as Samaritans training guidelines point out, whether under mental duress or not, ending one's life is in fact a choice, and persuading someone not to do has historically been seen as removal of agency.

The title Disconnected references a number of stories in the film in the way depression can engender a dissociative state whereby those experiencing it feel removed from themselves, as the lack of serotonin or dopamine becomes too much to bear, the deadening grey/blackness envelops, and sets subjective consciousness outside the individual, looking in at oneself. It also goes into how this is not always a permanent state, and how a person can recover, with patience, a strive towards balance and incremental optimistic steps. Medication is touched, but not lingered, upon. Daryl's story is particularly mesmerising, including a wrenching twist at the end.

In the year that the UK Chancellor of the Exchequer Jeremy Hunt announced £10 million to be given to the families of suicide cases for prevention and ease of suffering in his budget, producer Odette van Rensburg and co. have created a stylish, moving and perfectly paced testament to the causes and effects of this most silent of subjects.

27

Depp vs Heard + the End of Roe vs Wade:
Time for Some Rapprochement?

With the splintering of the media industry, mostly thanks to the Internet so far this century, a remedy was needed to keep the bucks coming in. One solution was, if not the invention, then the fanning of the flames of the culture wars. In the good ol' days of the good ol' legacy media, one voice was amplified to millions. With the brave new world of the Internet, a million voices shouted in ever-diminishing prevalence, increasingly at others who felt very similar to them.

Race and gender critical theory books had started to fill university library shelves at the end of the last century, as those in charge were now ready to play the long game of non-violent cultural revolution, realising that this kind of gradual behavioural influencing was the most effective way to lasting cultural change, whether publicly mandated or not.

Following repeated incidents of nations taking their citizens to wars that they could only experience through TV screens - and then only if they were on the winning side - the nature of experience was changing from real-time to meta-physical. Every news story, from the personal life of Bill Clinton to the 2008 financial crisis would result in wider cultural changes such as Occupy Wall Street, Anonymous and the #MeToo movement.

A surer way to keep the clicks coming was to create binary enemies in the shape of our fellow human beings, be they immigrants, people with non-conventional sexual preferences, or those seen as privileged or entitled. With populist movements, unwittingly and very wittingly encouraged by certain elements of the media, Operation Midland, the 'coming forward' culture of grievance and victimhood and Black Lives Matter became not just the cultural politics of yore, but the actual politics of now.

This new identity politics ignored what people were actually doing and their desire to live in the moment, and focussed on where they had come from, their distress about that and who they blamed for it all. The possibility that it was a million different factors and circumstances that made a situation was disregarded in the realisation that grievance-marketing needed to be as snappy and quickly digestible as any other aspect of mass-market advertising.

Johnny Depp had been an acting force of nature since What's Eating Gilbert Grape?, but had also long reminded of Jack White in his 'traditional role' interpretation of what he sees as a rock n' roll lifestyle. He's certainly got the eyes and hair for it. Any lack of familiarity with Amber Heard's work is more of a reflection of different generations rather than any comment on its quality. But the televised fight between them seemed generational. His rock n' roll traditionalism, including whisky and coke by all accounts, versus her fourth-wave feminism, media-supported entitlement, regardless of behaviour.

A great deal of the verdict mostly in Depp's favour seemed to indicate that it was mostly because his audience was bigger than hers, due to the fact that he'd been at the Hollywood game longer. This was clearly a toxic relationship between two actors, leading to violence and a degree of coercive control and extreme exasperation on both sides. The fact that they were both actors with identities heavily invested, in the twenty-first century moral climate, of being constantly in the right, meant that backing down in this adversarial blood-letting would be both very expensive and commercially suicidal.

The televised trial was actually a good deal more balanced than much UK mainstream reportage of such he said/she said situations, with most documentary producers drinking the received wisdom Kool-Aid of only representing the stance of the accuser, increasingly rarely if ever that of the accused. The fact is that conflict resolution, responsibly employed, could be used in the vast majority of domestic violence and known-party sexual assault allegations, as long as the bloodthirsty desire to send people to jail for human - as opposed to intentionally criminal - behaviour is reined in.

The same presumption of the gradual revolution the activists and academics had set in motion at the end of the last century was brought into further question by the ending of legal abortion in a number of US states, inveigled by ex-president Trump's installing of a number of traditionally-minded Republicans into the Supreme Court while he was in power. That no woman has ever had an abortion without a great deal of heartache and soul-searching was not in question.

What *was* in question, without the progressives seeming to realise it, was who got to choose the legality of this choice. Unwanted pregnancies would now go ahead, whether the woman liked it or not, unless she was so desperate as to go for an illegal backstreet termination. The machinery of democracy, as was seen in the Brexit wars in the UK in the late 2010s, can be painfully manipulated by the politically savvy. It's not all about for whom one votes; is also about how keen are those who lose on continuing to have an influence after the voting has stopped.

Rapprochement was a term used at the end of the World Wars of the twentieth century for working towards healing of formerly warring factions. Though more people are reportedly more anxious, stressed and depressed than ever, this must be more to do with the prevalence of screens in our lives than losing loved ones in violent circumstances, as those circumstances are statistically vanishingly rare, and decreasing.

The twenty-first century is a fifth of its way through; people consume more healthily and exercise more than ever, and are legally obliged to be more respectful with their words. There hasn't been a multilateral international world war for nearly a century, as more and more countries fall into the less-than-perfect but best-that-we-have basket of democracy.

Johnny and Amber were the very attractive, human faces of all these culture wars played out in a democratic court, shortly before the usually less-shrill traditionalists pulled the rug from under women's right to choose to legally continue with a pregnancy. Social progress isn't necessarily all in the direction of increasing liberalism, but all voices need to at least be seen to be heard in a true democracy. Freedom and healing will always eventually find a way, the lines of communication just need to be kept open, and the intention to listen to be kept in good faith.

28

The Opposite of Power is Harmony

If a British middle or upper-class girl strays outside her caste, she will be quietly and decisively punished. Society remains class-riven, and it's the great unmentionable in the culture wars. Just as it's the middle classes who are most likely to complain about the opposite sex or catastrophise about the environment, also will they chastise those who frolic beyond the guardrails.

An increasingly politicised aspect of so-called 'rape myths' is young women being encouraged not to take responsibility for their own behaviour. Consent in the age of convenience is a murky area, fought in case-by-case trials with *Tinder, Grindr* or *Plenty of Fish* as their background cultural contexts. Who wanted what, why were they there, and what were they going through when they did or did not choose to do something? Were they seduced, or persuaded? Did they regret something they weren't that enthusiastic about in the first place? When does that become anti-consensual?

And are new consent laws anti-biology? There is no equality in evolutionary biology, where the most efficient reproduction strategy prevails, regardless of human-wrought morality. This kind of natural struggle is otherwise known as the law of nature, and it sits uncomfortably with moral theorists. Nature will naturally dispose of the disabled or infirm, by disinterested parents unencumbered by too much nurturing scruples. Just like human beings before the twentieth century, they'd just move on and have another one (and bury the pain).

'Bad Character' aspects of 21st century sexual assault trials tacitly reference this absence of morality, establishing in court that the (usually male) defendant is habitually callous, uncaring, manipulative, untrustworthy, or otherwise 'immoral'. The moral character of the complainant is not tested in the same way, and pre-recorded video cross-examination means that there is no virtually no equality of arms in these allegations.

Is the fact that defendants are treated differently from complainants in terms of alcohol consumption a breach of the 2010 Equality Act? If both have been mutually, consensually drinking a similar amount as each other, the defendant can still be found liable of sexual assault or rape. Could it not be argued that this is discrimination on the basis of sex? This would mean that there should be an option to appeal based on incorrect original charge, for too many charges of rape or sexual assault being brought, due to activist pressure on the Ministry of Justice to drive up conviction rates.

Conventional Right and Left positions in sexual allegations are relatively recent stances in the area of sexual politics, with the Left once assuming that all allegedly predatory behaviour emanates from callous, uncaring, rightist types. However the situations of Harvey Weinstein, Russell Brand and a thousand other insufficiently risk-averse men across the arts has proven this to be untrue. Both the progressive-identifying and the traditional can be prostrate over the fire of eternal cancellation, dead or alive, contemporary or historical.

Objectivity and humanity are both possible at the same time however, as the decades-long race to the subjective bottom continues apace, leaving due judicial process flailing in its wake. The acknowledgement of what is means to be a human male, a testosterone-fuelled male - and the fact that none of these are either actually immoral or illegal - is forgotten in the flamethrower's arc.

Alpha/beta male definitions are reductive, as most males are as flexible as to their behaviours depending on social situation as any other survival-conscious creature. Silverback chest-beaters may proliferate in the football stadium and in the pub, but collaborate peacefully in the board room or workshop. Intelligent collaboration is as important to the socially-conscious male as it is to anybody else, and doesn't need to be viewed through the somewhat myopic prism of political feminism to justify itself.

The real difference is between integrated and disintegrated people, of both sexes. Diversity and inclusion policies celebrate a state of fractal disintegration, of many-sided beings flexing to their current mood or feeling, and celebrating this state of flux. Core consolidation or stability is ignored in favour of a mindful accepting of all good or bad circumstances and emotions, with the implication being that asserting opposition to such wispiness is somehow authoritarian.

This goes hand in hand with the neophilia surrounding us in the information age - the constant, profit-based celebration of the novel, however contradictory or once-immoral it might have seemed. Being overweight becomes body-positivity, being green becomes the ultimate moral good, and speaking to any young person about their sexual orientation or identity becomes outlawed as evil conversion therapy.

The concept of obedience has been rethought in this century to be the ultimate in immorality, indicating a feebleness of mind and sheeplike credulity, as opposed to the learning of good life lessons and following of wise tradition of all human community hitherto. Men can increasingly only talk about edgy culture if they're gay, and if they protest they are told in no uncertain terms they can MGTOW (Men Go Their Own Way). This can be out of choice, or out of psycho-spiritual necessity, as the political-feminist helmed media culture continues its white heteronormative pile-on.

Regarding the ever-present requirement to see all interactions through the glasses of Empathy, this would also logically involve seeing things from the perspective of the paedophile or psychopath; but that doesn't seem to be such a popular signal of virtue. Ultimately the progressive movement, fanned by the all-conquering algorithm, has been preoccupied with marginalising the mainstream, as if its autistic binary code is incapable of handling human nuance.

Philosophy has been preoccupied with power dynamics and relations since the discipline was conceptualised, from Plato to Nietzsche to Russell to Foucault. There are more things in heaven and earth than are dreamt of in this philosophy however, and human spirituality, properly recognised, thrives in harmony. This needn't be overtly positivistic, in a forced sense – it is innate.

All energies are attracted to the Golden Mean, or the median balance running through all inter-being relations. Power may dictate the political ebbs and flows of existence, and have always done so: what technology does with the still undefined spiritual force that runs through and around every thing needs to accommodate the magic of essential harmony for any co-existence to be possible in the long term.

29

The Ghosting of Laurence Fox

In September 2023, actor, presenter and leader of The Reclaim Party Laurence Fox was first suspended and then sacked from his own show on GB News. A week previously Fox had been invited onto fellow presenter Dan Wootton's show in the 9:30pm slot, and had arranged to discuss Ava-Santina Evans.

Evans, a Politics Joe reporter, had previously guested on the BBC's Politics Live program alongside Geoff 'Britain's only Tory comedian' Norcott, and appeared to belittle Norcott's heartfelt concern at suicide being the leading cause of death amongst men under fifty years of age. Clips of their exchange had been widely viewed on X and other platforms, which the self-described 'very emotional' Fox had seen.

After having had a couple of glasses of wine (according to a post-mortem interview on the Triggernometry podcast) Fox finished a mini-rant on the state of fourth wave feminism (henceforth 4WF) with the comment *'Who'd shag that?'* The comment was the sort that might happen around a million pub tables across the country; not so much on primetime terrestrial TV. As Fox semi-apologetically pointed out afterwards, the line between Zoom chat, podcasting, YouTube short and Ofcom-monitored commercial news show had become blurred – particularly for media figures increasingly used to ping-ponging between all formats - and numerous broadcasts were far more 'banterish' than this exchange.

It was an unnecessary and rude comment, but no less so that Evans' own public posting *'I'm not gonna shag you, mate'* on various online men's accounts. It was at least equalled by fellow Thespian Dame Joan Bakewell calling Fox a 'dick' on live TV, and two 4WFs avoiding the sack on BBC1's Have I Got News For You by asking each other if they'd shag him (in fairness the host said she probably would. Ava Evans, being not the unpresentable sort herself, may indeed also have received the attentions of the proudly heteronormative Fox in his more single days).

Why were the programmes on which Fox was commented about, in similar language, not disciplined as was he? Is the only defence that he said it first, so they were only responding? Pretty cynical, bad-faith stuff if that is the case. Fox often uses the phrase in his social messaging *'They are exactly what they accuse you of'*, pointing out the hypocrisy of the woke progressive movement (of which he likely considers 4WF a part). These double standards came only months after Fox reported that a BBC staffer had told him they wouldn't speak to him even if he won in the Uxbridge and Ruislip by-election.

It all goes back to when Fox went off-narrative to

call out what he saw as an audience member's racism on BBC1's Question Time in 2020, and refused to apologise for his 'immutable characteristics' - that of being a white, British heteronorm male. He immediately lost his representation without a word, and since then this again self-acknowledged 'privileged' actor has been the *bete-noir* of the mainstream media and what he sees as the excesses of woke.

Difficult journeys find friends however, and the Reverend Calvin Robinson was also sacked simply for standing by Fox after the latter's blanket condemnation in the media. Whether the reader likes the public facades of Fox and Robinson or not, this was a rare display of loyalty in the media, in a manner to which loyalty-barometer Jordan Peterson would (and did) approve.

There is a strange and quite new tactic employed by these 4WF types however. It almost seems premeditated in a media-training type of way, and it goes: call out (snitch); feign outrage (media messaging); claim victimhood (or have it claimed for you); ghost (ignore); move on to find new target. Whether it's the individual claiming victimhood for themselves or on behalf of others, whether it's Ava-Santina Evans, Evan Rachel Wood, Amber Heard, Charlotte Proudman or Jess Taylor, the path to moral/cultural dominance is in craven avoidance rather than dealing with the allegation in a frank, honest and direct manner. It's what would have in the olden days been called dishonourable behaviour.

This media-savvy strategy has metastasized to screens, pre-recorded evidence and possibly no more digital examinations of evidence in sexual assault trials in the Courts. Fox, like Andrew Tate, Peterson, Matt Walsh and many other public figures - male and female - is concerned about the emasculation of males and the feminisation of culture. This has ramped up over the 2013-2023 period, as Title IX has been industrialised in US universities, and Operation Soteria has radically lowered the bar for rape and sexual assault allegations in the UK.

The bolshie, gotcha attitude of physically attractive 4WF's in media culture is being used as a role model template for how this new breed of heavy-partying, super-successful victims should comport themselves in the public eye - and in keeping those algorigthmic £ £s rolling in. Political feminists have spent years plugging holes in leaky stories for lawsuits, professional tribunals and RASSO trials, and have made sure there is no argument possible for holding young women accountable for their actions in law, down to 'subjective knowing'.

Laurence Fox's lack of subjective knowing that his blokey chat with (gay) Dan Wootton would lead to a much longed for, if increasingly familiar, MSM demonisation doesn't count however. Wrong set of chromosomes.

30

Individualism

For many generations the term individualism has been equated with capitalism. Capitalism, the gathering of wealth in order to invest or save, has been equated with greed by socially-minded people who prioritise the apparent unfairness it can engender. But human beings are individuals, they are not money; nor are they those people around them, be that family or immediate community.

Groups lead to group-think, including insider-bias. This bias operates on the socio-human principle that we are right, and he/she is wrong, because he/she is not us. Overcoming this insider-bias - which is an intellectual failing - is a higher virtue, a true act of empathy. The free speech fallback 'I hate what you say but I'll defend to the death you right to say it' is classically based in this act of genuine empathy.

This kind of empathy has nothing to do with kindness. Tt's about elevating the mind out of base self-interest and strives to benefit all parties. This builds trust and respect, which is in turn good for the individual.

Terms like racist, sexist, homophobic and transphobic are neologisms, new words generally coined by social justice activists in the media. They are useful in promulgating political points, but meaningless in themselves. They are describing elements of the human psyche that have been relabelled immoral for the purposes of presumed 21st century social progress.

All animals have insider bias, as the unknown outsider may kill them and impregnate the females in their community. But human civilisation needs look beyond those evolutionary impulses to know that everyone is an outsider sometimes, so to imagine oneself as that all the time. This is how to engender a truly empathic state of mind.

An individual person isn't racist, as he or she treats the unknown other on their own qualities when it is individual meets individual. Even when they don't speak the same language, an international language of signs and meanings takes its place, and understanding grows. A group however can't actually be trusted to make the right decisions, even if democracy says that the voice of people is 'the Voice of God'. Populism is an easy thing to blame, but needs to be checked constantly for the base instincts of insider bias.

There is another saying, that you need to love yourself first before you can love others, and this is also true. Self-love is not narcissism, nor selfishness, nor arrogance; it is a positive characteristic. This has been ignored in 21st century social politics as unhelpful or somehow damaging to society, even while most people understand it to be true. This is because it is easier to blame others for our failings than take responsibility for them ourselves. This is why the ability to genuinely apologise is valuable, and vanishing. Apologising is an honourable thing, which has been relabelled in our mediated culture as weakness stemming from some degree of newly relabelled immorality.

Victimology has turned into a new form of McCarthyism. McCarthyism was a 'witch-hunt' carried out to expose alleged communists in mid 20th century US government. Claiming victimhood for alleged historical actions, or the behaviour of (usually) men in the present, has become its own currency. This currency is traded in media and compensation payouts, and future sympathy from activists schooled in the politicisation of sexual misadventure.

The individual is again attacked, as female tears bring automatic evolutionarily-honed sympathy - even if those tears are from the stress of the moment, rather than the alleged past actions themselves. The accused suddenly finds themselves with no friends beyond immediate family. This is a disempowering tactic, designed to create the impression of the 'lone wolf' in the dock, acting against the rules of the community.

A form of entitled positivity will then be employed by the accuser's supporters, bestowing praise on her for coming forward. The communal essence of gossip and shared sisterhood against the outsider lone operative comes into full effect, as a form of community policing comes into effect in the building of 'bad character' cases, in the absence of actual evidence. So while the individual is a threat to communist type states, so is he or she to the puritanical community.

This is a community that ignores the principle of 'let he who is without sin cast the first stone' in favour of insider-bias. Such ancient wisdom is problematic to the political morality of postmodernism, where all interpersonal relationships refer to power. So while the individual is on strong moral ground in being answerable only to his own conscience, and assuming that he isn't acting in bad faith, his existence is under existential threat within the endless subjectivity of postmodern culture.

The connection of the individual to capitalism has transmogrified to the connection to behavioural deviance, as a new lever towards societal compliance. Whether the poppies will be ever allowed to grow tall again in a liberal democratic west which appears to be crammed with Trojan Horses remains to be seen.

31

Free Speech and Agreed Terms

The majority of liberal-minded people in the West hold free speech as a sacred text, an Enlightenment value to rule them all. A central saying is *'I hate what you say, but I'll defend to the death your right to say it'*, often attributed to the poet Voltaire but actually originating from his biographer Evelyn Beatrice Hall, paraphrasing Voltaire's thinking.

There is an almost unassailable beauty in this phrase, and it reflects another central liberal democratic value – to *do as thou wilt*, as long as it doesn't harm anyone else. In our 21st century however, the concept of harm has been expanded by many self-declared progressives to include harmful words, leading to hate speech laws, and compelled speech to enforce them.

This has already culminated in prison sentences for some (teachers) and a battalion of lost jobs for others (academics). Shola Mos-B, a television commentator in the UK, essentially celebrated the Queen's death in 2022, leading many to wonder what sort if speech it was they were trying to keep free, and why. Mos isn't alone in her almost daily incites to racial disharmony, bringing every subject on which she is asked back to her perceived evils of colonialism.

The terrorist attack by Hamas on southern Israel on 7th October 2023, and that State's subsequent response, led to something of a watershed in free speech thinking. When does freedom of speech become freedom to protest, are they the same thing; and what of the harm done by a hundreds-strong Palestinian crowd utterly intimidating a tiny Foreign Legion stall, selling poppies for Remembrance Day?

Home Secretary Suella Braverman termed a Palestine-supporting 'million man march' - called for Remembrance Sunday - a 'hate march', scandalizing the media Left. These marchers had already dubbed Israel's response to October 7th a 'genocide', echoing trans activist India Willoughby's claim to the label a few months earlier when s/he heard about various governments disallowing males to compete in women's sports.

Genocide and suicide are the two go-to words for signifying panic that things aren't going your own way, when every moral fibre in your body is vibrating with indignation that others may not entirely agree with your moral certitude. Genocide for what others are doing to 'us', and suicide for how what others are doing to us makes us feel. They are linguistic levers of power, easily trendable and increasingly signifying nothing.

South African billionaire Elon Musk and British writer/comedian Andrew Doyle are both 'free speech absolutists', and there is a tacit agreement that free speech involves having to hear things that might disgust you. Even these two influential brains must feel the crack of the mad sometimes, however, as this disgust is worked up on a constant basis by bots on social media. This has become the greatest test of free speech - much like the populist and culture war struggles of the early 21st century have been liberal democracy's greatest tests. Douglas Murray, a British hero of the libertarian right, was forthright in his calling for the deportation of anyone displaying blatant antisemitism in a Triggernometry interview, openly telling the government *'I don't want them here'*.

So while there is the freedom to speak, and to protest, there is also an unwritten social code, which I call the doctrine of Agreed Terms. Since 2013 or thereabouts, the international left has been ramping up the pressure in intersectional grievance victimology, and changing language in law where they get the chance. From Occupy to #MeToo, Brexit to Black Lives Matter, Trump to Covid, no crisis has been wasted, with many suspected – and often proved - to have been thoroughly exploited to maximum advantage.

While the USA has its centuries-old Constitution, British law (devolved into the nations as it is) has one essential Agreed Term, almost its First Amendment: not to impose your ideology on another. For those growing up at the end of the 20th century, the social condition not to talk about religion or politics seemed staid and unnecessary, something holding progress back. The one way delivery of news and current affairs helped this status quo, and the then-establishment it all propped up.

With the advent of the 20th century, communication became multilateral, culminating in eight billion opinions expressible on X. Apparently much had been kept inside, and this was quickly weaponised by politicos of all interests, leading to huge profits due to algorithmically-inflamed posts and daily revelations of secrets kept. Liberal democracy's agreed terms were under assault by Mark Zuckerburg's *'move fast and break things'* ethos; this Bolshevik/futurist/punk spirit expressing itself in a self-righteous 'let's make the world a better place' post-storm.

Politeness, reserve, stoicism, sensibleness, centrism and adulthood were again seen as boring, repressive and old. As the 'singularity' of the internet approached – i.e. all things in the world being controlled by it – the core of the culture war was in this frank progress vs genteel traditionalism divide. To that frank progress could be added political feminism, critical race theory, trans activism, the green movement and cancel culture. To genteel traditionalism could be added populism, nationalism, individualism, conservatism, genetic theory and heredity.

Liberal democracy had been able to accommodate all these in the past, but a quarter of a century of global migration, plus internal media criticism, has led to a lack of confidence in the core. While the countries of the far East and the Islamic states were able to celebrate their own ethnic integrity, those of Europe of North America were not; and if they did, to be labelled far right, alt.right etc. The culture wars of the 2010s were a bellwether for events such as October 7th, where the Agreed Term idea of tolerance was stretched to breaking point, and pro-Palestinian activists screamed at the White House gates, and draped flags around Trafalgar Square.

Free speech can only exist in a global world which holds onto its tribal loyalties with a set of agreed terms which apply in the physical world. Say whatever you like on X, within the realms of decency (another agreed term); but the moment you leave the house, you're obliged by the long-established culture in which you live to queue, comment or joke about whatever you want - and leave the flags at home.

32

Evolutionary Biology vs the Progressive Future

The new establishment orthodoxy is hell-bent on the population becoming gender-fluid, mixed-heritage, vegan, environmentally-minded and agnostic.

This process is often termed cultural Marxism, as in the mass-saming of humanity in pursuit of equality, but Karl Marx would have been gobsmacked by the human fluidity we are being opted into, against our will, en-masse. This is social engineering mixed with political science, carried out unmandated on an international scale.

The original Marxism was twisted into Communism at the beginning of the 20th century in earnest, after experiments in France: and while the USSR version lasted for seventy years, and was the most notorious – its policies leaving at least as many dead as did World War II – it was the Chinese version which has been the most successful long term, showing a surprising flexibility.

This social engineering is at odds with evolutionary biology however, this discipline's most famous coiner,

Charles Darwin, being a near contemporary of Marx.

There is no equality of rights in biology, or equality of outcome. Biology is nature, humans are part of nature, and nature will always win in the end. We can modify the body and combat the terrors of disease, but change doesn't really happen either by accident or desire. Growth happens.

We become different beings as our trillions of cells die and are replaced by new ones, and are by dint of this process a fully new being every seven years. Sadly for some, there is no toggle switch to become the other sex, but we can accept who we are within the sex nature has assigned us, whatever those feelings.

Within these cells are ancient genetic codes dictating behaviours along the spectrum within one of the male/female binaries, exquisitely directing our impulses and behaviour on a primal-brain level. These observations are all uncontroversially established within biology, which is one of the sciences which cannot practically be postmodernised (though it is attempted).

Postmodernism is a cultural philosophy which has been applied to the arts and critical theory for over forty years, where essentially the person becomes more important than the thing they are thinking about, and is thus able to remake their world to the best of their desires.

This is why postmodern music is a mish-mash of many existing influences, postmodern art is more about ideas rather than decoration, and postmodern architecture tries to mix the old and the new (this is usually much more popular than the 'Brutalist' concrete structures of modernism).

While we can harness physics by means of engineering, and chemistry is already an almost endless process of refinement and discovery (see the pharmaceutical industry), biology is nature given - or God-given, to billions around the world.

So apply postmodern mixing, reality-defining principles to art and music all you like: it's fun, creatively challenging, and dynamic. But when applied to flesh and blood, the result may be thousands of people suing a sex-change clinic for choices they were told were more to do with their lifestyle choices than their mental health.

While beauty is in the eye of the beholder and individualism is important because we can't effectively take care of others without taking care of ourselves first, society can only function with a certain set of Agreed Terms.

In the postmodern West this is called consensus; but this is being steadily designed by elites in the thrall of social scientists who have decreed that technology has the answers to all life's woes.

Technology has many answers, but not those of the spirit either of people or of Gaia (a mystical term for the Earth as holistic concept). The real challenge for the rest of the 21st century isn't so much how to conquer primal human urges by technology or increasingly invasive laws, but in understanding, like adults, what is in our individual or collective control.

Nature as a force external to human beings doesn't need controlling beyond protecting ourselves from disease and extreme weather. Accepting ourselves as the complicated, spinning mess that we are would be the truly enlightened next phase of progress.

33

The New Religion of Identitarianism

So much of progressive politics is a child's idea of what the world should be. Environmental issues reduced to good vs evil narratives, interpersonal ones reduced to good women vs bad men, cultural problems reduced to All Religion Is Bad. People, and what goes on between them on micro and macro levels, are much more complicated than that.

Historically artists would have been relied upon to reflect and comment on this, but art and mental health have also been put into a co-morbid box where any deviance from art as therapy is met with imprecations to 'be kind'. Hot young women vs broken old men define the cultural sphere, where attractiveness bias is still very prevalent, the HYW led to believe anything they want is possible and the BOM correctly working out they've been utterly marginalised.

This new kind of victimology is an offshoot of the identitarian corruption increasingly prevalent in social media. Being any sort of victim is prized, along with a sort of 'stigmaphobia' encouraged within the new puritan classes. This is facilitated by a compliant news media, dependant on clicks and hits, exaggeration and omission its main currency. Outright lies are unnecessary and legally risky; it's easier for a half-competent hack to leave out unhelpful details or blow up the salacious details in any story.

Swallowing the progressive Kool-Aid is seen as a virtuous thing to do, and any cognisance of counter-narrative is seen as some sort of capitulation. Social media has presented false memories, revisionism and presentism as relevant and agreed academic theories, since their malleable subjectivity is attractive to wear. Any sense of Englishness and/or the importance of hidden nuance is forgotten as traditional, gammonish, out of date - as opposed to the fair, decent, long-termism of yore.

Safetyism and the damage done by litigation and apology-averse health and safety culture have extended deep roots into a what is otherwise a shallow, postmodern cultural surface. The individual and the nation state are as at-odds as ever, but the financial interests of the traditional left have been ignored in favour of this more lively identitarianism.

This *ignorist* ambivalence towards relatively recent political history follows a 'move fast and break things' ethos contained within Mark Zuckerburg and Elon Musk's Silicon Valley principles; itself an extension of futurist, rock n' roll and punk movements of the twentieth century. Alongside this revolutionary zeal, problematic terms such as transphobic, cis, hate speech etc. are smuggled into the media-youth lexicon, its verity established by left-leaning gender studies academics in higher education. 95% of these positions are occupied by the left-leaning, indicating the long march into the educational institutions: get 'em while they're young.

Hiroshima and Dolly the Sheep are two examples of technological progress that hasn't gone further in the public realm. Neither scientists nor the public want clones or nuclear war, so the 'progress' stopped there. Will that be the case for AI? Even virtual reality can't seem to get off the ground, on its fiftieth attempts.

Meghan Markle, Michelle Mone are two examples of the 'affirmations' comedown, as (mostly) women attempt to imagine themselves into a 'better future' – but better for whom exactly? Where do alleged governmental corruption, civic honours and identity political machinations become mandated by the public? Never, but social media creates the perception of a mandate, and that'll do for a generation that doesn't care much beyond what things *'look like'*.

The age of performative anonymity means that others' sympathy has become valued currency in place of the conventional 'success' narratives of the past. If you want to face the world as yourself, fine, but whistleblowing for the new morality is safer. Snitch culture is celebrated by these new puritans, while loyalty to friendship or traditions is seen as retrogressive or even immoral.

Social media messaging as performative art has replaced the conventional purpose of art as conduit and reflector for the multitude of humanity with an entrenched, stance-taking obstinacy. The sophisticated argument is put aside in favour of who can get their allegation in first, and who can set the narrative as what is good and what is bad.

Woke identitarianism is essentially religious in its ambivalent atheism/agnosticism. With belief in Christianity ever-diminishing, but the power of Islamism increasing, it's not Christianity that humanist rationalism need worry about so much any more. 'Belief' as opposed to the scientific method as the backstop to any debate is the problem. The ego-displacing route to this is the answer *'I don't know'*, which is the key sign of dialectic maturity. Identarianism still sees 'I don't know' as a sign of weakness and 'belief' as a strength – for now.

34

The New Moralities of British 'Social Justice'

Under 35s tend to see social media news as very serious - as long as it's about human rights - or else not serious at all. Over 35s tend to see it as baffling and very serious, but also not serious at all if the topic appears light to them.

While an older person might not see an eating disorder post as particularly crucial (*'just eat a meal, girl'*), younger 'digital natives' have been told that this is the moral meat of life itself. This feeds into a new value system which is as far from Abrahamic moralism as is atheism.

Words can now be 'non-crime hate incidents', their wielders sacked, cancelled, fined or imprisoned. If you are being harassed by people reporting your social media use, is there any comeback? This entirely depends on who gets their allegation in first. In tandem with the world becoming statistically less violent – possibly due to less lead and mercury in the water and air (see Steven Pinker)

- people are increasingly turning to rhetoric, allegation, offence and cancellation to silence 'the other side'.

The Postmasters scandal in the UK, in which more than 700 sub-postmasters were found to have been falsely accused due to Fujitsu's Horizon software, about which the authorities involved knew (many going to prison, some suicides) and nu-safetyism go hand in hand here. If something or someone is too expensive or rich to fail, any excuse will be found not to point the finger, even when it is clear to everyone where the system failure lies.

People like then-Post Office boss (and ordained vicar) Paula Vennells will use any excuse to see a project through, rather than point out the naked Emperor. This used to be called cowardice, now it's called damage limitation. If unquestionable tech becomes the new religion, then praying that it is infallible is as effective as any other kind of prayer. There is an obvious lesson in the Horizon affair in relation to the new PR rollout of artificial intelligence - humans must always be the final checker. When any one system becomes all-powerful we are in big trouble. righting system, as the Johnny Depp/Amber Heard case showed a pop culture world the reality of allegations of non-gendered domestic violence. Since then there have been exonerations of Kevin Spacey (twice), Andy Malkinson (after seventeen years wrongfully in prison), Brian Buckle and the Postmasters. Hollywood pull and ITV dramas help however, to the point of being absolutely necessary in the age of instant-response spectacle.

Exonerations since 2020 have actually been fairly positive in terms of a post-identitarian

Multitudes of Lords of the Stripes are at work on Britain's streets, as the nightmare of 'community policing' stalks the land, blithely self-important in its new woke application of the Equality Act. The main pre-crime suspects of these nu-laws tend to be indigenous Brits, gender critics and heteronormative males – the unholy trinity of the source of all socio-political ills. These new rozzers, often resplendent in Pride flags and Vogon-like legal decrees – however inaccurate or unlawful – seem to be the gender studies arm of the College of Policing, direct from trauma-informed seminars at Imperial College London.

Some particularly depressive progressives claim that humour, something which these community police people seem to abhor, is nothing more than a cover for wrongdoing, a mere projection. This new Thin Blue Line appears to be made up of such types, tearing up the social code in pursuit of their think-tanked version of social justice.

Rehabilitation from miscarriage of justice is never what justice reformers or rehabilitation professionals mean when they talk about being kind to prison-leavers. Justice reform is as woke-progressive an area as any other, but has difficulty countenancing that the law might be an ass until a number of newspaper front covers have featured the same story, i.e. Malkinson and the Postmasters. The 1400 other wrongful convictions per year (DPP Max Hill, 2019) can apparently go whistle.

Is men being forced to do courses for various kinds of alleged offending a form of genocide? If you take your cue from trans activists, Uiygar reporters or BBC headliner writers, it might as well be, so far has that 'ultimate wrong' term been stretched in recent years. By that measure it would be possible to construct fraud as the ultimate deviance in about 6 months, and have that replace the more salacious, headline-grabbing stories so familiar. It certainly can do much more, often hidden, damage.

Subjective human rights are everything to digital natives, the female half of which tend to be ideologically almost radical left. The males are more of a mixed bag – 'simps' who agree with the girls in order to get into their good books, and Andrew Tate fans on the other side of the wall - and that's just in the White West. All are apparently vulnerable to the ravages of social media bullying and harassment however, and the old adage of sticks and stones breaking bones but words never hurting has been apparently rendered redundant.

35

Art, Progressivism and Post-Woke Enlightenment

Art should have nothing to do with the progressive agenda, being as it is an incisive reflection of humanity, but it has increasingly been co-opted by charity or humanistic projects - and the more of that is incentivised, the more 'woke' it appears. The marginalisation of actual cutting-edge art goes along with this, as anything counter-narrative or truly 'disruptive' is quickly labelled 'conspiracy theory' or 'far right', these being the two favourite slurs of the progressive cultural media establishment.

Can art still really be 'anything goes'? In the postmodern melee the older have seen it all before, but the young care little about that, being more interested in the moral message behind the piece or the maker. Nick Cave has called this approach to artistic expression 'suffocating', and been put in the dinosaur bracket by some because of it.

Many artists and comedians privately agree with 'post-wokeism', or going beyond the current cultural impasse, but are afraid of their management and deals going awry if they are seen to go off-message. There is no rebellion or free-thought in this, which since art separated itself from the Church with the Renaissance, has been its raison-d'etre.

Without asking anyone's permission, news media has become the most important artform of the 21st century. Bad news sells, so the media look for ways to incentivise drama. It's not new, and not 'bad', it's just business. People online compromise their humanity with a moral image of themselves, avatars of reality. Should children learn again how to aspire and wait, for social media and other 'adult' privileges, as they have done for decades with smoking, sex, drinking, driving and voting?

Jonathan Haidt and Greg Lukianoff in the US have deep research on the damage being done to young minds by being permanently attached to demanding screens, and a sense of 'delayed satisfaction' needs to be inculcated - at least until when they have a bit more 'life-resilience' to handle social media's current intensity.

While news media has become the most impactful art, social media is the art we learned by accident. Temptations of its instant dopamine hit, the likes, the lights we want to deal with/turn off, and the new industry of crafting addictive sales posts in this new advertising space have led to ever more inventive approaches. The design, the psychology of sales, the response prediction and liveliness of this industry has pushed it into a vital competitive space - and traditional aesthetics have as much to do with it as they have in art for more than a hundred years.

Social media users are divided between those who take it very seriously and those who don't, but the latter still have a right to reply, and many on the progressive side resent this to the point of cancellation. Young left-leaning white women are being driven crazy by young left-leaning white women in the media. Young women are overwhelmingly more progressive; young men more traditional, or naturalistic.

'Grievance Intersectionality' is big business, makes money through clicks, and heads towards the sort of societal change craved by the (hard) left. The assumption must now be that people of colour in the media are anti-white heterodox, due to the sheer weight of that angle emanating from those people in all parts of the media. Due to all this intersectionality and incentivised progress, and an emphasis on being 'trauma-informed', Post-LGBTQ+ and pro-Palestine marches, Britain has reached the point where the police are feared but they're no longer respected.

Will the Next Big Thing be neurodiversity and criminal responsibility? *'It wasn't me your honour, it was my ADHD'* may turn out to be an extension of sick-note culture and the similarly incentivised mental health epidemic. It has never felt more likely that a post-technological revolution Enlightenment is around the corner.

If we can have the royal *we* why can't we have the non-binary *they*? Humanists UK now support this kind of inversion of linguistic-biological fact. Following the revelations of first the WPATH files and then the Cass report however, and the lasting damage knowingly done to young people, the mainstream is quickly reverse-ferreting. Whether this post-woke enlightenment will be reflected in genuine artistic expression - as happened in the first Enlightenment - remains to be seen.

36

Watching The Progressive Project

How would you feel if everything that you know as real in the world had been erased, replaced or inverted? This is an idea that is underway, the preparations having been made at the end of the last century and into this start of our current one.

There has been an academic tradition for some time on the Left of politics for the promotion of cultural revolution, and that then ushering in its political iteration. A version has been tried on a grand scale once before, in the shape of communism in the USSR between 1917 and 1989. This was socialism - in its totalitarian (Stalinist) form communism - and was originally based on the end of personal ownership of property.

More than one hundred years on from the Russian Revolution, the progressive movement is deeply into a quiet takeover of the institutions. Progressive theory takes the old model of economical socialism and moulds it into identity politics, supported by the writings of identity theorists of the last fifty years. As opposed to a colour-blind and gender-blind society as promoted by the 20th century version of multiculturalism, the progressive movement brings these identity definitions to the foreground.

Where once liberal democracy promoted the concept of global migration and integration, the progressives highlight accountability and reparations. Where once feminism was about the long march towards equality of opportunity for both sexes, progressive fourth-wave feminism promotes sex-work and the effective minimisation of men's rights. Where once it may have been said *'things were different back then'* or *'the past is a different country'*, the progressive movement supports the revision of historical works of art and literature, in order they be rewritten in a contemporaneously acceptable form.

Thus the passage of time itself offers no protection, as there is no statute of limitations in British law, and the moral barometer of now becomes more important than the cultural context of a work at the time it was made. So sensitivity readers, trigger warnings, autism-friendly performances (disability isn't forgotten by the progressive movement) and 'safe words' are all early flags for what has become known as cancel culture.

But it is not only in identity politics where the redesign is taking place. Fossil fuels have been under pressure for years now, replacing the long mass-marginalisation of smoking, which has led to that activity being relegated to hardy relaxation lovers shivering in outdoor smoking shelters. The push for electric cars, which contributed to making Elon Musk the world's richest man, has accompanied a relentless carnival of coordinated virtue-signalling in advertising and the media.

That there is not the infrastructure to get to 'Net Zero' anytime soon doesn't seem to deter the likes of pressure groups Just Stop Oil and Extinction Rebellion. This is the consequence of insistent doom-saying by certain newspapers and academics; David Attenborough,

Greta Thunberg and George Monbiot, catastrophising for a living since 2000 (a shorter timespan in young Thunberg's case). Former British Prime Minister Boris Johnson's wife Carrie pushed this to the top of agenda during her husband's three-year tenure, but the excesses of Net Zero's covert-leftist idealism was soon abandoned, in public anyway, by one of Johnson's successors Rishi Sunak.

Still, a look at the media messaging of any globalist organisation betrays a determined, almost hypnotised commitment to Net Zero, with absolutist green policies and transhumanism potentialities - gender transitioning, brain chips, and artificial intelligence. Leftists, ageing hippies and their CEO daughters at the tops of institutions have learned from Tony Blair's long march through the institutions (*'modernisation'*) and have learnt where they need to get to quietly push the levers of power.

The feminisation of this approach is multilateral; there is an understanding that many different bases need to be covered for the progressive revolution to be effective and deep-rooted. Graduates thus emerge from gender studies courses at universities staffed by 95% progressive educationalists, then quietly import their revolutionary learning into career progression in their new companies or organisations. The language used is cheerful, affirmatory, and checked for loopholes on a rolling basis. The revolutionary image of the past – donkey jackets, dungarees, black t-shirts and Doctor Martens – replaced by smart business suits, expensive hairdos and a subtly deployed, affable conformity.

The marginalisation of individualism is a necessity, and works first by creating insider-bias. The demasculation of society is again useful here, as the collaborative agreeableness of women can be used to ensure anyone – of either sex – sticking their heads above the parapet gets it instantly blown off. Make lone voices of protest uncool, unfashionable, eccentric, weird, perverted or somehow deviant. Make the traditional directness of men punishable with 'hate speech', bullying or even sexual harassment laws, and let women know they're also liable for individual thought by throwing the occasional lawsuit their way. Then make all of the above unsayable in public.

Historically speaking Marx cooked it up, Lenin brought it on, Blair made it smile and now Starmer will make any deviation from it impossible if not illegal. Political feminism has seen a chance to grab influence, as rates of male suicide are but a distraction from the main putsch, which is power. Suspicions that the WEF and CIA are involved on a medical-intelligence level are confirmed by truth-seeking journalists on a weekly basis.

Suspicions that social media is too wild a terrain for society to continue are confirmed with Online Safety laws. Public obedience is tested by means of coordinated health scares such as AIDS, Bird Flu, Sars and Covid; leading eventually to economy and mental health-decimating international lockdowns and new laws banning the right to protest. The nation state is the individual on a regional/racial level, is seen as a mortal threat to progress, and any insistence on national identity is stamped down upon as fascism or racism.

Meat-eating is seen as environmentally and morally destructive as fossil fuels, if not more so due to the mere thought of animals being killed, so the push to outlaw that is portmanteaued into the progressive brief under globally-supported veganism. Crime will vanish as the parameters of what is societally acceptable expand, and the ability to step outside of society's guardrails becomes practically impossible to do.

A global population of slaves to the elite is unlikely to be the aim, since those elites are liberally educated enough to see little value in material things, however many billions they have in the bank. They think they're acting quietly and systematically towards the moral betterment of the Earth and all the creatures on it, beyond material concerns. How much value they give to the variegated wholeness of the human experience, joyful consumption and the recognition of darkness as well as light being an integral part of the full tapestry of life remains to be seen.

ACKNOWLEDGEMENT

Everlasting thanks to: Dr Cheryl Allsop, Bettina Arndt, Matt Azoulay, Phil Baisley, JJ Barnes, Claire Best, George Bigwood, Rachel Billington MBE, Mike Bailey, James Barnett, Peter Boghossian, Mark Bradley, Sir Peter Bottomley MP, Brent Bowlby, Mike Buchanan, Will Burgess, Dr Ros Burnett, Sue Butler, John Casling, Nina Champion, Jonty Claypole, Francesca Cooney, Lady Val Corbett, Tilly Corke, Prof. Ben Crewe, Tim Crook, Tim Cruddas, Dora Dixon, Ellie Donaldson, Jeremy Dunning-Davies, Claire Dyer, Dr Dennis Eady, Tom Eagle, Can Erimtan, Karl Ertunc, Phil Faber, Janice Fiamengo, Juliet Fleming, Miles Fowler, Anne Fox, Baroness Claire Fox, Clive Freeman, David Macadam Freud, Margaret Gardener, Tony Gezi, Horatio Gooden, Patrick Graham, Nicki Gray, Nicholas Griffin, Neil Grutchfield, Stephen Halliday, Caroline Hammond, Will Harris, Paula Harriott, Claire Harrison, Dalton Harrison, Dnnis Hayes, Dr Louise Hewitt, Pat and Pete Hilder, Kirsten Howells, Enesa Ibrahimi, Erwin James, Prof. Jeffrey Ketland, Femi Laryea, Tim Heath, Steve Hodson, Sally James, Jackson Joseph, Jerome Joseph, Peter Joyce, Prof. Eric Kaufman, Jeffrey Ketland, Rosie Kinchen, Nicole Kulmaczewski, Fiona Larkin, Ben Leapman, Dr Sarah Lewis, Phil and Jane Lloyd, Tim Loughton MP, Dr Amy Ludlow, Greg Lukianoff, Kaz Lynch, Juliet Lyon CBE, Freya Lyons, Ruth McFarlane, Jimmy McGovern, Jim McSpirit, Dave Maguire, Simon Mayo, Anna and Pete Meecham, Jane Metcalfe, David Morgan, Katy Morgan-Davies, Julian Murdoch, Martin Nadin, Dr. Michael Naughton, Jules Nelson, Joseph Neuberger, Sally K. Norman, John Lee, Anne Marie and Ian Osborne, Caroline Pearce, Anita Phoenix, Juliet Pleming, Pete Pomerantsev, Christine Poole, Dave Potter, Sonia Poulton, Brenda Rayner, John Richards, Ade Rowbottom, Soruche Saajedi, Jody Sabral, Bethany Schmidt, Fina Schneider, Hazel Scully, David Sedaris, Barry Sheerman MP, Becky Simmons, Anoeushka Smith, Sue Stephens, Russell Spencer, Faith Spear, Sue Stephens, Felicity Stryjak, Fehmi Suda, Jo Tapp, Louis Theroux, Jennifer Thetford-Kay, Holly Thomas, Alex Thomson, Camilla Tominey, Joey Tsang, Warwick and Jackie Turnbull, Camilla Tominey, Richard Vobes, Calum Walker, Emma Wells, Jo Wheeler, Joanna Williams, Helena Wysocki, Liz Yeld, Paul Yoward

ABOUT THE AUTHOR

Sean Bw Parker

Sean Bw Parker (MA) is a British writer, artist and musician, born in Exeter in 1975. He gained a Masters degree in Fine Art from the University for the Creative Arts in 2003, following which he lived in Istanbul for ten years until 2014, where he gave TEDx talk 'Stammering and Creativity' and also lectured at Istanbul University. He has published several books, poems, albums and paintings, and won a number of awards.

He has been published in Westminster Commission reports, T.S. Eliot Foundation, Time Out Istanbul, Louder Than War, and appeared at the Brighton Science Festival, the University of Bristol, BIMM and others. He has interviewed Julie Burchill, Ed Harcourt, Kristin Hersh, Ian Broudie of The Lightning Seeds and Sarah Blackwood of Dubstar, hosted shows by The Members, Mark Morriss of The Bluetones and Eat Static at his Seafish music and arts venue in 2016, and was interviewed for a Sky Arts documentary in the same year. He curated the Chi-Signs, Blakefest and Wildefest mini-festivals between 2015 and 2017, and has been involved with numerous other exhibitions and live events.

BOOKS BY THIS AUTHOR

All Books By Sean Bw Parker

Compelling Speech – The Stammering Enigma (2023)
States of Independence: From Pop Art to Art Rock and Beyond (2022)
Bean Soup (2018)
Swimming Uphill: Absurd Theories (2017)
The Cougar and The Silver Fox (illustrated poem, 2017)
Devils of Bognor (2016)
Genuflecting Before the Pork-Barrel Demagogues (2015)
Salt in the Milk – Ten Years in Istanbul (2014)

Printed by Amazon Italia Logistica S.r.l.
Torrazza Piemonte (TO), Italy